Coventry Patmore

The Unknown Eros

Coventry Patmore

The Unknown Eros

ISBN/EAN: 9783744688192

Printed in Europe, USA, Canada, Australia, Japan

Cover: Foto ©Thomas Meinert / pixelio.de

More available books at **www.hansebooks.com**

THE

UNKNOWN EROS.

BY

COVENTRY PATMORE.

I.—XLVI.

" Deliciæ meæ esse cum filiis hominum."—PROV. VIII. 31.

LONDON:

GEORGE BELL AND SONS, YORK STREET,

COVENT GARDEN.

1878.

CONTENTS.

VII.—A FAREWELL.

VIII.—VICTORY IN DEFEAT.

IX.—WIND AND WAVE.

X.—LEGEM TUAM DILEXI.

XI.—THE TOYS.

XII.—PSYCHE.

XIII.—TRISTITIA.

XIV.—MAGNA EST VERITAS.

I.

PROEM.

" MANY speak wisely, some inerrably :

Witness the beast who talk'd that should have bray'd,

And Caiaphas that said

' Expedient 'twas for all that One should die' ;

But what avails

When Love's right accent from their wisdom fails,

And the Truth-criers know not what they cry !

Say, wherefore thou,

B

As under bondage of some bitter vow,

Warblest no word,

When all the rest are shouting to be heard?

Why leave the fervid running just when Fame

'Gan whispering of thy name

Amongst the hard-pleased Judges of the Course?

Parch'd is thy crystal-flowing source?

Pierce, then, with thought's steel probe the trodden ground

Till passion's buried floods be found;

Intend thine eye

Into the dim and undiscover'd sky

Whose lustres are the pulsings of the heart,

And promptly, as thy trade is, watch to chart

The lonely suns, the mystic hazes and throng'd sparkles
     bright

That, named and number'd right

In sweet transpicuous words, shall glow alway

With Love's three-stranded ray,

Red wrath, compassion golden, lazuline delight."

Thus, in reproof of my despondency,-

My Mentor; and thus I :

O, season strange for song!

And yet some timely Power persuades my lips.

Is't England's parting soul that nerves my tongue

As other Kingdoms, nearing their eclipse,

Have, in their latest bards, uplifted strong

The voice that was their voice in earlier days?

Is it her sudden, loud and piercing cry,

The note which those that seem too weak to sigh

Will sometimes utter just before they die?

Lo, weary of the greatness of her ways,

There lies my Land, with hasty pulse and hard,

Her ancient beauty marr'd,

And, in her cold and aimless roving sight,

Horror of light;

Sole vigor left in her last lethargy,

PROEM.

Save when, at bidding of some dreadful breath,

The rising death

Rolls up with force;

And then the furiously gibbering corse

Shakes, panglessly convuls'd, and sightless stares,

Whilst one Physician pours in rousing wines,

One anodynes,

And one declares

That nothing ails it but the pains of growth.

   My last look loth

Is taken; and I turn, with the relief

Of knowing that my life-long hope and grief

Are surely vain,

To that unshapen time to come, when She,

A dim, heroic Nation long since dead,

The foulness of her agony forgot,

Shall all benignly shed

Through ages vast

The ghostly grace of her transfigured past

Over the present, harass'd and forlorn,

Of nations yet unborn;

And this shall be the lot

Of those who, in the bird-voice and the blast

Of her omniloquent tongue,

Have truly sung

Or greatly said,

To shew as one

With those who have best done,

And be as rays,

Thro' the still altering world, around her changeless head.

　　Therefore no 'plaint be mine

Of listeners none,

No hope of render'd use or proud reward,

In hasty times and hard;

But chants as of a lonely thrush's throat—

At latest eve,

PROEM.

That does in each calm note

Both joy and grieve;

Notes few and strong and fine,

Gilt with sweet day's decline,

And sad with promise of a different sun.

'Mid the loud concert harsh

Of this fog-folded marsh,

To me, else dumb,

Uranian Clearness, come!

Give me to breathe in peace and in surprise

The light-thrill'd ether of your rarest skies,

Till inmost absolution start

The welling in the grateful eyes,

The heaving in the heart.

Winnow with sighs

And wash away

With tears the dust and stain of clay,

Till all the Song be Thine, as beautiful as Morn,

Bedeck'd with shining clouds of scorn;

And Thou, Inspirer, deign to brood

O'er the delighted words, and call them Very Good.

This grant, Clear Spirit; and grant that I remain

Content to ask unlikely gifts in vain.

II.

THE UNKNOWN EROS.

WHAT rumour'd heavens are these

Which not a poet sings,

O, Unknown Eros? What this breeze

Of sudden wings

Speeding at far returns of time from interstellar space

To fan my very face,

And gone as fleet,

Through delicatest ether feathering soft their solitary beat,

With ne'er a light plume dropp'd, nor any trace

To speak of whence they came, or whither they depart?

And why this palpitating heart,—

This blind and unrelated joy,

This meaningless desire,

That moves me like the Child

Who in the flushing darkness troubled lies,

Inventing lonely prophecies,

Which even to his Mother mild

He dares not tell;

To which himself is infidel;

His heart not less on fire

With dreams impossible as wildest Arab Tale,

(So thinks the boy,)

With dreams that turn him red and pale,

Yet less impossible and wild

Than those which bashful Love, in his own way and hour,

Shall duly bring to flower?

O, Unknown Eros, sire of awful bliss,

What portent and what Delphic word,

Such as in form of snake forbodes the bird,

Is this ?

In me life's even flood

What eddies thus ?

What in its ruddy orbit lifts the blood

Like a perturbed moon of Uranus

Reaching to some great world in ungauged darkness hid ;

And whence

This rapture of the sense

Which, by thy whisper bid,

Reveres with obscure rite and sacramental sign

A bond I know not of nor dimly can devine ;

This subject loyalty which longs

For chains and thongs

Woven of gossamer and adamant,

To bind me to my unguess'd want,

And so to lie,

Between those quivering plumes that thro' fine ether

    pant,

For hopeless, sweet eternity?

What God unhonour'd hitherto in songs,

Or which, that now

Forgettest the disguise

That Gods must wear who visit human eyes,

Art Thou?

Thou art not Amor; or, if so, yon pyre,

That waits the willing victim, flames with vestal fire;

Nor mooned Queen of maids; or, if thou'rt she,

Ah, then, from Thee

Let Bride and Bridegroom learn what kisses be!

In what veil'd hymn

Or mystic dance

Would he that were thy Priest advance

Thine earthly praise, thy glory limn?

Say, should the feet that feel thy thought

In double-center'd circuit run,

In that compulsive focus, Nought,

In this a furnace like the sun ;

And might some note of thy renown

And high behest

Thus in enigma be express'd :

" There lies the crown

" Which all thy longing cures.

" Refuse it, Mortal, that it may be your's !

" It is a Spirit, though it seems red gold ;

" And such may no man, but by shunning, hold.

" Refuse it, though refusing be despair ;

" And thou shalt feel the phantom in thy hair."

III.

THE DAY AFTER TO-MORROW.

PERCHANCE she droops within the hollow gulf

Which the great wave of coming pleasure draws,

Not guessing the glad cause !

Ye Clouds that on your endless journey go,

Ye Winds that westward flow,

Thou heaving Sea

That heav'st 'twixt her and me,

Tell her I come ;

Then only sigh your pleasure, and be dumb;

For the sweet secret of our either self

We know.

Tell her I come,

And let her heart be still'd.

One day's controlled hope, and then one more,

And on the third our lives shall be fulfill'd !

Yet all has been before.

Palm placed in palm, twin smiles, and words astray.

What other should we say ?

But shall I not, with ne'er a sign, perceive,

Whilst her sweet hands I hold,

The myriad threads and meshes manifold

Which Love shall round her weave :

The pulse in that vein making alien pause

And varying beats from this ;

Down each long finger felt, a differing strand

Of silvery welcome bland ;

And in her breezy palm

And silken wrist,

Beneath the touch of my like numerous bliss

Complexly kiss'd,

A diverse and distinguishable calm ?

What should we say !

It all has been before ;

And yet our lives shall now be first fulfill'd,

And into their summ'd sweetness fall distill'd

One sweet drop more ;

One sweet drop more, in absolute increase

Of unrelapsing peace.

  O, heaving Sea

That heav'st as if for bliss of her and me,

And separatest not dear heart from heart,

Though each 'gainst other beats too far apart,

For yet awhile

Let it not seem that I behold her smile.

O, weary Love, O, folded to her breast,

Love in each moment years and years of rest,

Be calm, as being not.

Ye oceans of intolerable delight,

The blazing photosphere of central Night,⌒

Be ye forgot.

Terror, thou swarthy Groom of Bride-bliss coy,

Let me not see you toy.

O, Death, too tardy with thy hope intense

Of kisses close beyond conceit of sense;

O, Life, too liberal, while to take her hand

Is more of hope than heart can understand;

Perturb my golden patience not with joy,

Nor, through a wish, profane

The peace that should pertain

To him who does by her attraction move.

Has all not been before?

One day's controlled hope, and one again,

And then the third, and ye shall have the rein,

O Life, Death, Terror, Love ! ⁓

But soon let your unrestful rapture cease,

Ye flaming Ethers thin,

Condensing till the abiding sweetness win

One sweet drop more ;

One sweet drop more in the measureless increase

Of honied peace.

IV.

" LET BE !"

Ah, yes; we tell the good and evil trees

By fruits: but how tell these ?

Who does not know

That good and ill

Are done in secret still,

And that which shews is verily but show !

How high of heart is one, and one how sweet of mood :

But not all height is holiness,

Nor every sweetness good :

And grace will sometimes lurk where who could guess

The Critic of his kind,

Dealing to each his share,

With easy humour, hard to bear,

May not impossibly have in him shrined,

As in a gossamer globe or thickly padded pod,

Some small seed dear to God.

Haply yon wretch, so famous for his falls,

Got them beneath the Devil-defended walls

Of some high Virtue he had vow'd to win ;

And that which you and I

Call his besetting sin

Is but the fume of his peculiar fire

Of inmost contrary desire,

And means wild willingness for her to die,

Dash'd with despondence of her favour sweet ;

He fiercer fighting, in his worst defeat,

Than I or you,

That only courteous greet

Where he does hotly woo,

Did ever fight, in our best victory.

Another is mistook

Through his deceitful likeness to his look !

Let be, let be :

Why should I clear myself, why answer thou for me ?

That shaft of slander shot

Miss'd only the right blot.

I see the shame

They cannot see :

'Tis very just they blame

The thing that's not.

V.

THE CONTRACT.

Twice thirty centuries and more ago,
All in a heavenly Abyssinian vale,
Man first met woman; and the ruddy snow
On many-ridgëd Abora turn'd pale,
And the song choked within the nightingale.
A mild white furnace in the thorough blast
Of purest spirit seem'd She as she pass'd;
And of the Man enough that this be said,
He look'd her Head.

Towards their bower

Together as they went,

With hearts conceiving torrents of content,

And linger'd prologue fit for Paradise,

He, gathering power

From dear persuasion of the dim-lit hour

And doubted sanction of her sparkling eyes,

Thus supplicates her conjugal assent,

And thus she makes replies :

" Lo, Eve, the Day burns on the snowy height,

But here is mellow night !"

" Here let us rest.   The languor of the light

Is in my feet.

It is thy strength, my Love, that makes me weak ;

Thy strength it is that makes my weakness sweet.

What would thy kiss'd lips speak ?"

" See, what a world of roses I have spread

To make the bridal bed.

Come, Beauty's self and Love's, thus to thy throne be led!"

" My Lord, my Wisdom, nay!

Does not yon love-delighted Planet run,

(Haply against her heart,)

A space apart

For ever from her strong-persuading Sun?

O say,

Shall we no voluntary bars

Set to our drift?   I, Sister of the Stars,

And Thou, my glorious, course-compelling Day!"

" Yea, yea!

Was it an echo of her coming word

Which, ere she spake, I heard?

Or through what strange distrust was I, her Head,

Not first this thing to have said?

Alway

Speaks not within my breast

The uncompulsive, great and sweet behest

Of something bright,

Not named, not known, and yet more manifest

Than is the morn,

The sun being just at point then to be born ?

O, Eve, take back thy ' Nay.'

Trust me, Belov'd, ever in all to mean

Thy blissful service, sacrificial, keen ;

But bondless be that service, and let speak—"

    " This other world of roses in my cheek,

Which hide them in thy breast, and deepening seek

That thou decree if they mean Yea or Nay."

    " Did e'er so sweet a word such sweet gainsay !"

    " And when I lean, Love, on you, thus, and smile

So that my Nay seems Yea,

You must the while

Thence be confirm'd that I deny you still."

    " I will, I will !"

    " And when my arms are round your neck, like this,

And I, as now,

Melt like a golden ingot in your kiss,

Then, more than ever, shall your splendid word

Be as Archangel Michael's severing sword?

Speak, speak!

Your might, Love, makes me weak,

Your might it is that makes my weakness sweet."

   "I vow, I vow!"

   "And are you happy, O, my Hero and Lord;

And is your joy complete?"

   "Yea, with my joyful heart my body rocks,

And joy comes down from heaven in floods and shocks,

As from Mount Abora comes the avalanche."

   "My Law, my Light!

Then am I yours as your high mind may list.

No wile shall lure you, none can I resist!"

   Thus the first Eve

With much enamour'd Adam did enact

Their mutual free contract

Of virgin spousals, blissful beyond flight

Of modern thought, with great intention staunch,

Though unobliged until that binding pact.

Whether She kept her word, or He the mind

To hold her, wavering, to his own restraint,

Answer, ye pleasures faint,

Ye fiery throes, and upturn'd eyeballs blind

Of sick-at-heart Mankind,

Whom nothing succour can,

Until a heaven-caress'd and happier Eve

Be join'd with some glad Saint

In like espousals, blessed upon Earth,

And She her Fruit forth bring ;

No numb, chill-hearted, shaken-witted thing,

'Plaining his little span,

But of proud virgin joy the appropriate birth,

The Son of God and Man.

VI.

PEACE.

O ENGLAND, how hast thou forgot,

In dullard care for undisturb'd increase

Of gold, which profits not,

The gain which once thou knew'st was for thy peace!

Honour is peace, the peace which does accord

Alone with God's glad word:

"My peace I send you, and I send a sword."

O England, how hast thou forgot,

How fear'st the things which make for joy, not fear,

Confronted near.

Hard days?　'Tis what the pamper'd seek to buy

With their most willing gold in weary lands.

Loss and pain risk'd?　What sport but understands

These for incitements!　Suddenly to die,

With conscience a blurr'd scroll?

The sunshine dreaming upon Salmon's height

Is not so sweet and white

As the most heretofore sin-spotted soul

That darts to its delight

Straight from the absolution of a faithful fight.

Myriads of homes unloosen'd of home's bond,

And fill'd with helpless babes and harmless women fond?

Let those whose pleasant chance

Took them, like me, among the German towns,

After the war that pluck'd the fangs from France,

With me pronounce

Whether the frequent black, which then array'd

Child, wife, and maid,

Did most to magnify the sombreness of grief,

Or add the beauty of a staid relief

And freshening foil

To cheerful-hearted Honour's ready smile!

    Beneath the heroic sun

Is there then none

Whose sinewy wings by choice do fly

In the fine mountain-air of public obloquy,

To tell the sleepy mongers of false ease

That war's the ordained way of all alive,

And therein with goodwill to dare and thrive

Is profit and heart's peace?

    But in his heart the fool now saith :

"The thoughts of Heaven were past all finding out,

Indeed, if it should rain

Intolerable woes upon our land again,

After so long a drought!"

" Will a kind Providence our vessel whelm,

With such a pleasant pilot at the helm?"

" Or let the throats be cut of pretty sheep

That care for nought but pasture rich and deep?"

" Were 't Evangelical of God to deal so foul a blow

At people who hate Papists so?"

" What, make or keep

A tax for ship and gun,

When 'tis full three to one

Yon bully but intends

To beat our friends?"

" Let's put aside

Our costly pride.

Our appetite's not gone

Because we've learn'd to doff

Our caps, where we were used to keep them on."

" If times get worse,

We've money in our purse,

And patriots that know how, let who will scoff,

To buy our perils off.

Yea, blessed in our midst

Art thou who lately didst,

So cheap,

The old bargain of the Saxon with the Dane."

Thus in his heart the fool now saith ;

And, lo, our trusted leaders trust fool's luck,

Which, like the whale's 'mazed chine,

When they thereon were mulling of their wine,

Will some day duck.

Remnant of Honour, brooding in the dark

Over your bitter cark,

Staring, as Rispah stared, astonied seven days,

Upon the corpses of so many sons,

Who loved her once,

Dead in the dim and lion-haunted ways,

Who could have dreamt

That times should come like these !

Prophets, indeed, taught lies when we were young,

And people loved to have it so ;

For they teach well who teach their scholars' tongue !

But that the foolish both should gaze,

With feeble, fascinated face,

Upon the wan crest of the coming woe,

The billow of earthquake underneath the seas,

And sit at ease,

Or stand agape,

Without so much as stepping back to 'scape,

Mumbling, " Perchance we perish if we stay :

'Tis certain wear of shoes to stir away !"

Who could have dreamt

That times should come like these !

Remnant of Honour, tongue-tied with contempt,

Consider; you are strong yet, if you please.

A hundred just men up, and arm'd but with a frown,

May hoot a hundred thousand false loons down,

Or drive them any way like geese.

But to sit silent now is to suborn

The common villany you scorn.

In the dark hour

When phrases are in power,

And nought's to choose between

The thing which is not and which is not seen,

One fool, with lusty lungs,

Does what a hundred wise, who hate and hold their
tongues,

Shall ne'er undo.

In such an hour,

When eager hands are fetter'd and too few,

And hearts alone have leave to bleed,

Speak; for a good word then is a good deed.

VII.

A FAREWELL.

WITH all my will, but much against my heart,

We two now part.

My Very Dear,

Our solace is, the sad road lies so clear.

It needs no art,

With faint, averted feet

And many a tear,

In our opposed paths to persevere.

Go thou to East, I West.

We will not say

There's any hope, it is so far away.

But, O, my Best,

When the one darling of our widowhead,

The nursling Grief,

Is dead,

And no dews blur our eyes

To see the peach-bloom come in evening skies,

Perchance we may,

Where now this night is day,

And even through faith of still averted feet,

Making full circle of our banishment,

Amazed meet;

The bitter journey to the bourne so sweet

Seasoning the termless feast of our content

With tears of recognition never dry.

VIII.

VICTORY IN DEFEAT.

Ah, God, alas,

How soon it came to pass

The sweetness melted from thy barbed hook

Which I so simply took;

And I lay bleeding on the bitter land,

Afraid to stir against thy least command,

But losing all my pleasant life-blood, whence

Force should have been heart's frailty to withstand.

Life is not life at all without delight,

Nor has it any might;

And better than the insentient heart and brain

Is sharpest pain;

And better for the moment seems it to rebel,

If the great Master, from his lifted seat,

Ne'er whispers to the wearied servant " Well !"

Yet what returns of love did I endure,   ·

When to be pardon'd seem'd almost more sweet

Than aye to have been pure !

But day still faded to disastrous night,

And thicker darkness changed to feebler light,

Until forgiveness, without stint renew'd,

Was now no more with loving tears imbued,

Vowing no more offence.

Not less to thine Unfaithful didst thou cry,

" Come back, poor Child; be all as 'twas before."

But I,

" No, no; I will not promise any more !

Yet, when I feel my hour is come to die,

And so I am secured of continence,

Then may I say, though haply then in vain,

'My only, only Love, O, take me back again !' "

Thereafter didst thou smite

So hard that, for a space,

Uplifted seem'd Heav'n's everlasting door,

And I indeed the darling of thy grace.

But, in some dozen changes of the moon,

A bitter mockery seem'd thy bitter boon.

The broken pinion was no longer sore.

Again, indeed, I woke

Under so dread a stroke

That all the strength it left within my heart

Was just to ache and turn, and then to turn and ache,

And some weak sign of war unceasingly to make.

And here I lie,

With no one near to mark,

Thrusting Hell's phantoms feebly in the dark,

And still at point more utterly to die.

O, God, how long!

Put forth indeed thy powerful right hand,

While time is yet,

Or never shall I see the blissful land !"

    Thus I: then God, in pleasant speech and strong,

(Which soon I shall forget) :

" The man who, though his fights be all defeats,

Still fights,

Enters at last

The heavenly Jerusalem's rejoicing streets

With glory more, and more triumphant rites

Than always-conquering Joshua's, when his blast

The frighted walls of Jericho down cast;

And, lo, the glad surprise

Of peace beyond surmise,

More than in common Saints, for ever in his eyes."

IX.

WIND AND WAVE.

THE wedded light and heat,

Winnowing the witless space,

Without a let,

What are they till they beat

Against the sleepy sod, and there beget

Perchance the violet !

Is the One found,

Amongst a wilderness of as happy grace,

To make Heaven's bound;

So that in Her

All which it hath of sensitively good

Is sought and understood

After the narrow mode the mighty Heavens prefer?

She, as a little breeze

Following still Night,

Ripples the spirit's cold, deep seas

Into delight;

But, in a while,⁄

The immeasurable smile

Is broke by fresher airs to flashes blent

With darkling discontent;

And all the subtle zephyr hurries gay,

And all the heaving ocean heaves one way,

'Tward the void sky-line and an unguess'd weal;

Until the vanward billows feel

The agitating shallows, and devine the goal,

And to foam roll,

And spread and stray

And traverse wildly, like delighted hands,

The fair and fleckless sands ;

And so the whole

Unfathomable and immense

Triumphing tide comes at the last to reach

And burst in wind-kiss'd splendours on the deaf'ning
    beach,

Where forms of children in first innocence

Laugh and fling pebbles on the rainbow'd crest

Of its untired unrest.

X.

LEGEM TUAM DILEXI.

THE " Infinite." Word horrible! at feud

With life, and the braced mood

Of power and joy and love;

Forbidden, by wise heathen ev'n, to be

Spoken of Deity,

Whose Name, on popular altárs, was " The Unknown,"

Because, or ere It was reveal'd as One

Confined in Three,

LEGEM TUAM DILEXI.

The people fear'd that it might prove

Infinity,

The blazon which the devils desired to gain ;

And God, for their confusion, laugh'd consent ;

Yet did so far relent,

That they might seek relief, and not in vain,

In dashing of themselves against the shores of pain.

Nor bides alone in hell

The bond-disdaining spirit boiling to rebel.

But for compulsion of strong grace,

The pebble in the road

Would straight explode,

And fill the ghastly boundlessness of space.

The furious power,

To soft growth twice constrain'd in leaf and flower,

Protests, and longs to flash its faint self far

Beyond the dimmest star.

The same

Seditious flame,

Beat backward with reduplicated might,

Struggles alive within its stricter term,

And is the worm.

And the just Man does on himself affirm

God's limits, and is conscious of delight,

Freedom and right,

And so His Semblance is, Who, every hour,

By day and night,

Buildeth new bulwarks 'gainst the Infinite.

For, ah, who can express

How full of bonds and simpleness

Is God,

How narrow is He,

And how the wide waste field of possibility

Is only trod

Straight to His homestead in the human heart,

And all His art

Is as the babe's, that wins his Mother to repeat

Her little song so sweet!

What is the chief news of the Night?

Lo, iron and salt, heat, weight and light

In every star that drifts on the great breeze!

And these

Mean Man,

Darling of God, Whose thoughts but live and move

Round him; Who woos his will

To wedlock with His own, and does distil

To that drop's span

The attar of all rose-fields of all love!

Therefore the soul select assumes the stress

Of bonds unbid, which God's own style express

Better than well,

And aye hath borne,

To the Clown's scorn,

The fetters of the threefold golden chain:

Narrowing to nothing all his worldly gain ;

(Howbeit in vain ;

For to have nought

Is to have all things without care or thought !)

Surrendering, abject, to his equal's rule,

As though he were a fool,

The free wings of the will ;

(More vainly still ;

For none knows rightly what 'tis to be free—

But only he

Who, vow'd against all choice, and fill'd with awe

Of the ofttimes dumb or clouded Oracle,

Does wiser than to spell,

In his own suit, the least word of the Law !)

And lastly bartering life's dear bliss for pain ;

But evermore in vain ;

For joy (rejoice ye Few that tasted have !)

Is Love's obedience

Against the genial laws of natural sense,

Whose wide, self-dissipating wave,

Prison'd in artful dykes,

Trembling returns and strikes

Thence to its source again,

In backward billows fleet,

Crest crossing crest ecstatic as they greet ;

Thrilling each vein,

Exploring every chasm and cove

Of the full heart with floods of honied love,

And every principal street

And obscure alley and lane

Of the intricate brain

With brimming rivers of light and breezes sweet

Of the primordial heat ;

Till, unto view of me and thee,

Lost the intense life be,

Or ludicrously display'd, by force

Of distance, as a soaring eagle, or a horse

On far-off hillside shewn,

May seem a gust-driv'n rag or a dead stone.

Nor by such bonds alone—

But more I leave to say,

Fitly revering the Wild Ass's bray

Also his hoof,

Of which, go where you will, the marks remain

Where the religious walls have hid the bright reproof.

XI.

THE TOYS.

My little Son, who look'd from thoughtful eyes,

And moved and spoke in quiet grown-up wise,

Having my law the seventh time disobey'd,

I struck him, and dismiss'd

With hard words and unkiss'd,

His Mother, who was patient, being dead.

Then, fearing lest his grief should hinder sleep,

I visited his bed,

But found him slumbering deep,

With darken'd eyelids, and their lashes yet

From his late sobbing wet.

And I, with moan,

Kissing away his tears, left others of my own;

For, on a table drawn beside his head,

He had put, within his reach,

A box of counters and a red-vein'd stone,

A piece of glass abraded by the beach

And six or seven shells,

A bottle with bluebells

And two French copper coins, ranged there with carefu

    art,

To comfort his sad heart.

So when that night I pray'd

To God, 1 wept, and said:

Ah, when at last we lie with tranced breath,

Not vexing Thee in death,

And Thou rememberest of what toys

We made our joys,

How weakly understood,

Thy great commanded good,

Then, fatherly not less

Than I whom Thou hast moulded from the clay,

Thou'lt leave Thy wrath, and say,

" I will be sorry for their childishness."

XII.

PSYCHE.

WHATE'ER thou dost thou'rt dear!

Uncertain troubles sanctify

That magic well-spring of the willing tear,

Thine eye.

Thy jealous fear,

With not the rustle of a rival near;

Thy careless disregard of all

My tenderest care;

Thy dumb despair

When thy keen wit my worship may construe

Into contempt of thy divinity;

They please me too!

But should it once befall

These accidental charms to disappear,

Leaving withal

Thy sometime self the same throughout the year,

So glowing, grave and shy,

Kind, talkative and dear,

As now thou sitt'st to ply

The fireside tune

Of that neat engine deft at which thou sew'st

With fingers mild and foot like the new moon,

O, in what speech of honey, milk and gold,

Could my content be told!

Forget, then, (but I know

Thou canst not so,)

Thy customs of some prædiluvian state.

I am no Bullfinch, fair my Butterfly,

That thou should'st try

Those zigzag courses, in the welkin clear;

Nor cruel Boy that, fledd'st thou straight

Or paused, mayhap

Might catch thee, for thy colours, with his cap.

XIII.

TRISTITIA.

DARLING, with hearts conjoin'd in such a peace

That Hope, so not to cease,

Must still gaze back,

And count, along our love's most happy track,

The landmarks of like inconceiv'd increase,

Promise me this :

If thou alone should'st win

God's perfect bliss,

And I, beguiled by gracious-seeming sin,

Say, loving too much thee,

Love's last goal miss,

And any vows may then have memory,

Never, by grief for what I bear or lack,

To mar thy joyance of heav'n's jubilee.

Promise me this;

For else I should be hurl'd,

Beyond just doom

And by thy deed, to Death's interior gloom,

From the mild borders of the banish'd world

Wherein they dwell

Who builded not unalterable fate

On pride, fraud, envy, cruel lust or hate;

Yet loved too laxly sweetness and heart's ease,

And strove the creature more than God to please.

For such as these

Loss without measure, sadness without end !

Yet not for this do thou disheaven'd be

With thinking upon me.

Though black, when scann'd from heaven's surpassing

    bright,

This might mean light,

Foil'd with the dim days of mortality.

For God is everywhere.

Go down to deepest Hell, and He is there,

And, as a true but quite estranged Friend,

He works, 'gainst gnashing teeth of devilish ire,

With love deep hidden lest it be blasphemed,

If possible, to blend

Ease with the pangs of its inveterate fire ;

Yea, in the worst

And from His Face most wilfully accurst

Of souls in vain redeem'd,

He does with potions of oblivion kill

Remorse of the lost Love that helps them still.

Apart from these,

Near the sky-borders of that banish'd world,

Wander pale spirits among willow'd leas,

Lost beyond measure, sadden'd without end,

But since, while erring most, retaining yet

Some ineffectual fervour of regret,

Retaining still such weal

As spurned Lovers feel,

Preferring far to all the world's delight

Their loss so infinite,

Or Poets, when they mark

In the clouds dun

A loitering flush of the long sunken sun,

And turn away with tears into the dark.

Know, Dear, these are not mine

But Wisdom's words, confirmed by divine

Doctors and Saints, though fitly seldom heard

Save in their own prepense-occulted word,

Lest fools be fool'd the further by false hope,

And wrest sweet knowledge to their own decline;

And (to approve I speak within my scope)

The Mistress of that dateless exile grey

Is named in surpliced Schools *Tristitia*.

But, O, my Darling, look in thy heart and see

How unto me,

Secured of my prime care, thy happy state,

In the most unclean cell

Of sordid Hell,

And worried by the most ingenious hate,

It never could be anything but well,

Nor from my soul, full of thy sanctity,

Such pleasure die

As the poor harlot's, in whose body stirs

The innocent life that is and is not hers:

Unless, alas, this fount of my relief

By thy unheavenly grief

Were closed.

So, with a consecrating kiss,

And hearts made one in past all previous peace,

And bosoms thus opposed,

Promise me this !

XIV.

MAGNA EST VERITAS.

HERE, in this little Bay,
Full of tumultuous life and great repose,
Where, twice a day,
The purposeless, glad ocean comes and goes,
Under high cliffs, and far from the huge town,
I sit me down.
For want of me the world's course will not fail:
When all its work is done, the lie shall rot;
The truth is great, and shall prevail,
When none cares whether it prevail or not.

XV.

DEPARTURE.

It was not like your great and gracious ways!
Do you, that have nought other to lament,
Never, my Love, repent
Of how, that July afternoon,
You went,
With sudden, unintelligible phrase,
And frighten'd eye,
Upon your journey of so many days,

Without a single kiss or a good-bye ?

I knew, indeed, that you were parting soon ;

And so we sate, within the low sun's rays,

You whispering to me, for your voice was weak,

Your harrowing praise.

Well, it was well, my Wife,

To hear you such things speak,

And see your love

Make of your eyes a growing gloom of life,

As a warm South-wind sombres a March grove.

And it was like your great and gracious ways

To turn your talk on daily things, my Dear,

Lifting the luminous, pathetic lash

To let the laughter flash,

Whilst I drew near,

Because you spoke so low that I could scarcely hear.

But all at once to leave me at the last,

More at the wonder than the loss aghast,

With huddled, unintelligible phrase,

And frighten'd eye,

And go your journey of all days

With not one kiss or a good-bye,

And the only loveless look the look with which you

    pass'd,

'Twas all unlike your great and gracious ways.

XVI.

THE STANDARDS.

THAT last,

Blown from our Zion of the Seven Hills,

Was no uncertain blast !

Listen : the warning all the champaign fills,

And minatory murmurs, answering, mar

The Night, both near and far,

Perplexing many a drowsy citadel

Beneath whose ill-watch'd walls the Powers of Hell,

With armed jar

And angry threat, surcease

Their long-kept compact of contemptuous peace !

Lo, yonder, where our little English band,

With peace in heart and wrath in hand,

Have dimly ta'en their stand,

Sweetly the light

Shines from the solitary peak at Edgbaston,

'Whence, o'er the dawning Land,

Gleam the gold blazonries of Love irate

'Gainst the black flag of Hate.*

Envy not, little band,

Your brothers, under the Hohenzollern hoof

Put to the splendid proof.

Your hour is near !

The spectre-haunted time of idle Night,

---

* This Ode was written in the year 1874, soon after the publication
of an incendiary pamphlet against the English Catholics.

Your only fear,

Thank God, is done,

And Day and War, Man's work-time and delight,

Begun.

    Ho, ye of the van there, veterans great of cheer,

Look to your footing, when, from yonder verge,

The wish'd Sun shall emerge;

Lest once again the Flower of Sharon bloom

After a way the Stalk call heresy.

Strange splendour and strange gloom

Alike confuse the path

Of customary faith;

And when the dim-seen mountains turn to flame

And every roadside atom is a spark,

The dazzled sense, that used was to the dark,

May well doubt, " Is't the safe way and the same

By which we came

From Egypt, and to Canaan mean to go?"

But know,

The clearness then so marvellously increas'd,

The light'ning shining through the West and East,

Is the great promised sign

Of His victorious and divine

Approach, whose coming in the clouds shall be,

As erst was His humility,

A stumbling unto some, the first-bid to the Feast.

   Cry, Ho!

Good speed to them that come and them that go

From either gathering host,

And, after feeble, false allegiance, now first know

Their post.

Ho, ye

Who loved our Flag

Only because there flapp'd none other rag

Which gentlemen might doff to, and such be,

'Save your gentility!

For leagued, alas, are we

With many a faithful rogue

Discrediting bright Truth with dirt and brogue;

And flatterers, too,

That still would sniff the grass

After the 'broider'd shoe,

And swear it smelt like musk where He did pass,

Though he were Borgia or Caiaphas.

Ho, ye

Who dread the bondage of the boundless fields

Which Heaven's allegiance yields,

And, like to house-hatch'd finches, hop not free

Unless 'tween walls of wire,

Look, there be many cages : choose to your desire !

Ho, ye,

Of God the least belov'd, of Man the most,

That like not leaguing with the lesser host,

Behold the invested Mount,

And that assaulting Sea with ne'er a coast.

You need not stop to count!

   But come up, ye

Who adore, in any way,

Our God by His wide-honour'd Name of YEA.

Come up; for where ye stand ye cannot stay.

Come all

That either mood of heavenly joyance know,

And, on the ladder hierarchical,

Have seen the order'd Angels to and fro

Descending, with the pride of service sweet,

Ascending, with the rapture of receipt!

Come who have felt, in soul and heart and sense,

The entire obedience

Which opes the bosom, like a blissful wife,

To the Husband of all life!

Come ye that find contentment's very core

In the light store

And daisied path

Of Poverty,

And know how more

A small thing that the righteous hath

Availeth than the ungodly's riches great.

Come likewise ye

Which do not yet disown as out of date

That brightest third of the dead Virtues three,

Of Love the crown elate

And daintiest glee !

Come up, come up, and join our little band.

Our time is near at hand.

The sanction of the world's undying hate

Means more than flaunted flags in windy air.

Be ye of gathering fate

Now gladly ware.

Now from the matrix, by God's grinding wrought,

The brilliant shall be brought ;

The white stone mystic set between the eyes

Of them that get the prize;

Yea, part and parcel of that mighty Stone

Which shall be thrown

Into the Sea, and Sea shall be no more.

XVII.

"IF I WERE DEAD."

"If I were dead, you'd sometimes say, Poor Child!"

The dear lips quiver'd as they spake,

And the tears brake

From eyes which, not to grieve me, brightly smiled.

Poor Child, poor Child!

I seem to hear your laugh, your talk, your song.

It is not true that Love will do no wrong.

Poor Child!

And did you think, when so you cried and smiled,

How I, in lonely nights, should lie awake,

And of those words your full avengers make?

Poor Child, poor Child!

And now, unless it be

That sweet amends thrice told are come to thee,

O, God, have thou *no* mercy upon me!

Poor Child!

XVIII.

EURYDICE.

Is this the portent of the day nigh past,

And of a restless grave

O'er which the eternal sadness gathers fast?

Or but the heaped wave

Of some chance, wandering tide,

Such as that world of awe

Whose circuit, listening to a foreign law,

Conjunctures ours at unguess'd dates and wide,

Does in the Spirit's tremulous ocean draw,

To pass unfateful on, and so subside ?

Thee, whom ev'n more than Heaven loved I have,

And yet have not been true

Even to thee,

I, dreaming, night by night seek now to see,

And, in a mortal sorrow, still pursue

Thro' sordid streets and lanes

And houses brown and bare

And many a haggard stair

Ochrous with ancient stains,

And infamous doors, opening on hapless rooms,

In whose unhaunted glooms

Dead pauper generations, witless of the sun,

Their course have run ;

And ofttimes my pursuit

Is check'd of its dear fruit

By things brimful of hate, my kith and kin,

Furious that I should keep

Their forfeit power to weep,

And mock, with living fear, their mournful malice

    thin.

But ever, at the last, my way I win

To where, with perfectly sad patience, nurst

By sorry comfort of assured worst,

Ingrain'd in fretted cheek and lips that pine,

On pallet poor

Thou lyest, stricken sick,

Beyond love's cure,

By all the world's neglect, but chiefly mine.

Then sweetness, sweeter than my tongue can tell,

Does in my bosom well,

And tears come free and quick

And more and more abound

For piteous passion keen at having found,

After exceeding ill, a little good ;

A little good

Which, for the while,

Fleets with the current sorrow of the blood,

Though no good here has heart enough to smile.

XIX.

REMEMBERED GRACE.

SINCE succour to the feeblest of the wise

Is charge of nobler weight

Than the security

Of many and many a foolish soul's estate,

This I affirm,

Though fools will fools more confidently be :

Whom God does once with heart to heart befriend,

He does so till the end ;

And having planted life's miraculous germ,

One sweet pulsation of responsive love,

He sets him sheer above,

Not sin and bitter shame

And wreck of fame,

But Hell's insidious and more black attempt,

The envy, malice and pride,

Which men who share so easily condone

That few ev'n list such ills as these to hide.

From these unalterably exempt

Through the remember'd grace

Of that divine embrace,

Of his sad errors none,

Though gross to blame,

Shall cast him lower than the cleansing flame,

Nor make him quite depart

From the small flock named " after God's own heart,"

And to themselves unknown.

G

Nor can he quail

In faith, nor flush nor pale

When all the other idiot people spell

How this or that new prophet's word belies

Their last high oracle ;

But constantly his soul

Points to its pole

Ev'n as the needle points, and knows not why ;

And, under the ever-changing clouds of doubt,

When others cry,

" The stars, if stars there were,

" Are quench'd and out !"

To him, uplooking t'ward the hills for aid,

Appear, at need display'd,

Gaps in the low-hung gloom, and, bright in air,

Orion or the Bear.

XX.

SEMELE.

No praise to me!

My joy 'twas to be nothing but the glass

Thro' which the general boon of Heaven should pass,

To focus upon thee.

Nor is't thy blame

Thou first should'st glow, and, after, fade i' the flame.

It takes more might

Than God has given thee, Dear, so long to feel delight.

Shall I, alas,

Reproach thee with thy change and my regret?

Blind fumblers that we be

About the portals of felicity !

The wind of words would scatter, tears would wash

Quite out the little heat

Beneath the silent and chill seeming ash,

Perchance, still slumbering sweet.

XXI.

CREST AND GULF.

Much woe that man befalls

Who does not run when sent, nor come when Heaven calls;

But whether he serve God, or his own whim,

Not matters, in the end, to any one but him;

And he as soon

Shall map the other side of the Moon,

As trace what his own deed,

In the next chop of the chance gale, shall breed.

This he may know :

His good or evil seed⁓

Is like to grow,

For its first harvest, quite to contraries :

The father wise

Has still the hare-brain'd brood ;

'Gainst evil, ill example better works than good ;

The poet, fanning his mild flight

At a most keen and arduous height,

Unveils the tender heavens to horny human eyes

Amidst ingenious blasphemies.

Wouldst raise the poor, in Capuan luxury sunk ?

The Nation lives but while its Lords are drunk !

Or spread Heav'n's partial gifts o'er all, like dew ?

The Many's weedy growth withers the gracious Few !

Strange opposites, from those, again, shall rise.

Join, then, if thee it please, the bitter jest⁓

Of mankind's progress ; all its spectral race

Mere impotence of rest,

The heaving vain of life which cannot cease from self,

Crest altering still to gulf

And gulf to crest

In endless chace

That leaves the tossing water anchor'd in its place!

Ah, well does he who does but stand aside,

Sans hope or fear,

And marks the crest and gulf in station sink and rear.

And prophesies 'gainst trust in such a tide :

For he sometimes is prophet, heavenly taught,

Whose message is that he sees only nought!

Nathless, discern'd may be,

By listeners at the doors of destiny,

The fly-wheel swift and still

Of God's incessant will,

Mighty to keep in bound, tho' powerless to quell,

The amorous and vehement drift of man's herd to hell.

XXII.

PROPHETS WHO CANNOT SING.

Ponder, ye Just, the scoffs that frequent go
From forth the foe:
"The holders of the Truth in Verity
Are people of a harsh and stammering tongue!
The hedge-flower hath its song;
Meadow and tree
Water and wandering cloud
Find Seers who see,

And, with convincing music clear and loud,

Startle the adder-deafness of the crowd

By tones, O Love, from thee.

Views of the unveil'd heavens alone forth bring

Prophets who cannot sing,

Praise that in chiming numbers will not run ;

At least, from David until Dante, none,

And none since him.

Fish, and not swim ?

They think they somehow should, and so they try ;

But (haply 'tis they screw the pitch too high)

'Tis still their fates

To warble tunes that nails might draw from slates.

Poor Seraphim !

They mean to spoil our sleep, and do, but all their

    gains

Are curses for their pains !"

   Now who but knows

That truth to learn from foes

Is wisdom ripe ?

Therefore no longer let us stretch our throats

Till hoarse as frogs

With straining after notes

Which but to touch would burst an organ-pipe.

Far better be dumb dogs.

XXIII.

FELICIA.

Of infinite Heaven the rays,

Piercing some eyelet in our cavern black,

Ended their viewless track

On thee to smite

Solely, as on a diamond stalactite,

And in mid-darkness lit a rainbow's blaze,

Wherein the absolute Reason, Power, and Love,

That erst could move

Mainly in me but toil and weariness,

Renounced their deadening might,

Renounced their undistinguishable stress

Of withering white,

And did with gladdest hues my spirit caress,

Nothing of Heaven in thee showing infinite,

Save the delight.

XXIV.

TIRED MEMORY.

The stony rock of death's insensibility
Well'd yet awhile with honey of thy love,
And then was dry;
Nor could thy picture, nor thine empty glove,
Nor all thy kind, long letters, nor the band
Which really spann'd
Thy body chaste and warm
Henceforward move

Upon the stony rock their wearied charm.

At last, then, thou wast dead.

Yet would I not despair,

But wrought my daily task, and daily said

Many and many a fond, unfeeling prayer,

To keep my vows of faith to thee from harm.

In vain.

" For 'tis," I said, " all one,

" The wilful faith, which has no joy or pain,

" As if 'twere none."

Then look'd I miserably round

If aught of duteous love were left undone,

And nothing found.

But, kneeling in a Church, one Easter-Day,

It came to me to say :

" Though there is no intelligible rest,

" In Earth or Heaven,

" For me, but on her breast,

" I yield her up, again to have her given,

" Or not, as, Lord, thou wilt, and that for aye."

And the same night, in slumber lying,

I, who had dream'd of thee as sad and sick and dying,

And only so, nightly for all one year,

Did thee, my own most Dear,

Possess

In gay, celestial beauty nothing coy,

And felt thy soft caress

With heretofore unknown reality of joy.

But, in our mortal air,

None thrives for long upon the happiest dream,

And fresh despair

Bade me seek round afresh for some extreme

Of unconceiv'd, interior sacrifice

Whereof the smoke might rise

To God, and 'mind him that one pray'd below.

And so,

In agony, I cried :

" My Lord, if thy strange will be this,

" That I should crucify my heart,

" Because my love has also been my pride,

" I do submit, if I saw how, to bliss

" Wherein She has no part."

And I was heard,

And taken at my own remorseless word.

O, my most Dear,

Was't treason, as I fear?

'Twere that, and worse, to plead thy veiled mind,

Kissing thy babes, and murmuring in mine ear,

" Thou canst not be

" Faithful to God, and faithless unto me !"

Ah, prophet kind !

I heard, all dumb and blind

With tears of protest ; and I cannot see

But faith was broken.   Yet, as I have said,

My heart was dead,

Dead of devotion and tired memory,

When a strange grace of thee

In a fair stranger, as I take it, bred

To her some tender heed,

Most innocent

Of purpose therewith blent,

And pure of faith, I think, to thee; yet such

That the pale reflex of an alien love,

So vaguely, sadly shown,

Did her heart touch

Above

All that, till then, had woo'd her for its own.

And so the fear, which is love's chilly dawn,

Flush'd faintly upon lids that droop'd like thine,

And made me weak,

By thy delusive likeness doubly drawn,

And Nature's long suspended breath of flame

H

TIRED MEMORY.

Persuading soft, and whispering Duty's name,

Awhile to smile and speak

With this thy Sister sweet, and therefore mine;

Thy Sister sweet,

Who bade the wheels to stir

Of sensitive delight in the poor brain,

Dead of devotion and tired memory,

So that I lived again,

And, strange to aver,

With no relapse into the void inane,

For thee;

But (treason was't?) for thee and also her.

XXV.

"FAINT YET PURSUING."

Heroic Good, target for which the young
Dream in their dreams that every bow is strung,
And, missing, sigh
Unfruitful, or as disbelievers die,
Thee having miss'd, I will not so revolt,
But lowlier shoot my bolt,
And lowlier still, if still I may not reach,
And my proud stomach teach

That less than highest is good, and may be high.

An even walk in life's uneven way,

Though to have dreamt of flight and not to fly

Be strange and sad,

Is not a boon that's given to all who pray.

If this I had

I'd envy none !

Nay, trod I straight for one

Year, month or week,

Should Heaven withdraw, and Satan me amerce

Of power and joy, still would I seek

Another victory with a like reverse ;

Because the good of victory does not die,

As dies the failure's curse,

And what we have to gain

Is, not one battle, but a weary life's campaign.

Yet meaner lot being sent

Should more than me content ;

Yea, if I lie

Among vile shards, though born for silver wings,

In the strong flight and feathers gold

Of whatsoever heavenward mounts and sings

I must by admiration so comply

That there I should my own delight behold.

Yea, though I sin each day times seven,

And dare not lift the fearfullest eyes to Heaven,

Thanks must I give

Because that seven times are not eight or nine,

And that my darkness is all mine,

And that I live

Within this oak-shade one more minute even,

Hearing the winds their Maker magnify.

XXVI.

PAIN.

O, PAIN, Love's mystery,

Close next of kin

To joy and heart's delight,

Low Pleasure's opposite,

Choice food of sanctity

And medicine of sin,

Angel, whom even they that will pursue

Pleasure with hell's whole gust

Find that they must

Perversely woo,

My lips, thy live coal touching, speak thee true.

Thou sear'st my flesh, O Pain,

But brand'st for arduous peace my languid brain,

And bright'nest my dull view,

Till I, for blessing, blessing give again,

And my roused spirit is

Another fire of bliss,

Wherein I learn

Feelingly how the pangful purging fire

Shall furiously burn

With joy, not only of assured desire,

But also present joy

Of seeing the life's corruption, stain by stain,

Vanish in the clear heat of Love irate,

And, fume by fume, the sick alloy

Of luxury, sloth and hate

Evaporate;

Leaving the man, so dark erewhile,

The mirror merely of God's smile.

Herein, O Pain, abides the praise

For which my song I raise;

But even the bastard good of intermittent ease

How greatly doth it please!

With what repose

The being from its bright exertion glows

When from thy strenuous storm the senses sweep

Into a little harbour deep

Of rest;

When thou, O Pain,

Having devour'd the nerves that thee sustain,

Sleep'st, till thy tender food be somewhat grown again;

And how the lull

With tear-blind love is full!

What mockery of a man am I express'd

That I should wait for thee

To woo !

Nor even dare to love, till thou lov'st me.

How shameful, too,

Is this :

That, when thou lov'st, I am at first afraid

Of thy fierce kiss,

Like a young maid ;

And only trust thy charms

And get my courage in thy throbbing arms.

And, when thou partest, what a fickle mind

Thou leav'st behind,

That, being a little absent from mine eye,

It straight forgets thee what thou art,

And ofttimes my adulterate heart

Dallies with Pleasure, thy pale enemy.

O, for the learned spirit without attaint

That does not faint,

But knows both how to have thee and to lack,

And ventures many a spell,

Unlawful but for them that love so well,

To call thee back.

XXVII.

THE TWO DESARTS.

Not greatly moved with awe am I

To learn that we may spy

Five thousand firmaments beyond our own.

The best that's known

Of the heavenly bodies does them credit small.

View'd close, the Moon's fair ball

Is of ill objects worst,

A corpse in Night's highway, naked, fire-scarr'd,
accurst;

And now they tell

That the Sun is plainly seen to boil and burst

Too horribly for hell.

So, judging from these two,

As we must do,

The Universe, outside our living Earth,

Was all conceiv'd in the Creator's mirth,

Forecasting at the time Man's spirit deep,

To make dirt cheap.

Put by the Telescope!

Better without it man may see,

Stretch'd awful in the hush'd midnight,

The ghost of his eternity.

Give me the nobler glass that swells to the eye

The things which near us lie,

Till Science rapturously hails,

In the minutest water-drop,

A torment of innumerable tails.

These at the least do live.

But rather give

A mind not much to pry

Beyond our royal-fair estate

Betwixt these desarts blank of small and great.

Wonder and beauty our own courtiers are,

Pressing to catch our gaze,

And out of obvious ways

Ne'er wandering far.

XXVIII.

DELICIÆ SAPIENTIÆ DE AMORE.

Love, light for me

Thy ruddiest blazing torch,

That I, albeit a beggar by the Porch

Of the glad Palace of Virginity,

May gaze within, and sing the pomp I see;

For, crown'd with roses all,

'Tis there, O Love, they keep thy festival!

But first warn off the beatific spot

Those wretched who have not

Even afar beheld the shining wall,

And those who, once beholding, have forgot,

And those, most vile, who dress

The charnel spectre drear

Of utterly dishallow'd nothingness

In that refulgent fame,

And cry, Lo, here !

And name

The Lady whose smiles inflame

The sphere.

Bring, Love, anear,

And bid be not afraid

Young Lover true, and love-foreboding Maid,

And wedded Spouse, if virginal of thought ;

For I will sing of nought

Less sweet to hear

Than seems

A music in their half-remember'd dreams.

   The magnet calls the steel:

Answers the iron to the magnet's breath;

What do they feel

But death!

The clouds of summer kiss in flame and rain,

And are not found again;

But the heavens themselves eternal are with fire

Of unapproach'd desire,

By the aching heart of Love, which cannot rest,

In blissfullest pathos so indeed possess'd.

O, spousals high;

O, doctrine blest,

Unutterable in even the happiest sigh;

This know ye all

Who can recall

With what a welling of indignant tears

Love's simpleness first hears

The meaning of his mortal covenant,

And from what pride comes down

To wear the crown

Of which 'twas very heaven to feel the want.

How envies he the ways

Of yonder hopeless star,

And so would laugh and yearn

With trembling lids eterne,

Ineffably content from infinitely far

Only to gaze

On his bright Mistress's responding rays,

That never know eclipse ;

And, once in his long year,

With præternuptial ecstacy and fear,

By the delicious law of that ellipse

Wherein all citizens of ether move,

With hastening pace to come

Nearer, though never near,

His Love

And always inaccessible sweet Home ;

There on his path doubly to burn,

Kiss'd by her doubled light

That whispers of its source,

The ardent secret ever clothed with Night,

Then go forth in new force

Towards a new return,

Rejoicing as a Bridegroom on his course !

This know ye all ;

Therefore gaze bold,

That so in you be joyful hope increas'd,

Thorough the Palace portals, and behold

The dainty and unsating Marriage-Feast.

O, hear

Them singing clear

" Cor meum et caro mea" round the " I am,"

The Husband of the Heavens, and the Lamb

Whom they for ever follow there that kept,

Or, losing, never slept

Till they reconquer'd had in mortal fight

The standard white.

O, hear

From the harps they bore from Earth, five-strung, what

    music springs,

While the glad Spirits chide

The wondering strings !

And how the shining sacrificial Choirs,

Offering for aye their dearest hearts' desires,

Which to their hearts come back beatified,

Hymn, the bright aisles along,

The nuptial song,

Song ever new to us and them, that saith,

" Hail Virgin in Virginity a Spouse !"

Heard first below

Within the little house

At Nazareth;

Heard yet in many a cell where Brides of Christ

Lie hid, emparadised,

And where, although

By the hour 'tis night,

There's light,

The Day still lingering in the lap of snow.

Gaze and be not afraid

Ye wedded few that honour, in sweet thought

And glittering will,

So freshly from the garden gather still

The lily sacrificed;

For ye, though self-suspected here for nought,

Are highly styled

With the thousands twelve times twelve of undefiled.

Gaze and be not afraid

Young Lover true and love-foreboding Maid.

The full noon of deific vision bright

Abashes nor abates

No spark minute of Nature's keen delight.

'Tis there your Hymen waits!

There where in courts afar all unconfused they crowd,

As fumes the starlight soft

In gulfs of cloud,

And each to the other, well-content,

Sighs oft,

" 'Twas this we meant!"

Gaze without blame

Ye in whom living Love yet blushes for dead shame.

There of pure Virgins none

Is fairer seen,

Save One,

Than Mary Magdalene.

Gaze without doubt or fear

Ye to whom generous Love, by any name, is dear.

Love makes the life to be

A fount perpetual of virginity ;

For, lo, the Elect

Of generous Love, how named soe'er, affect

Nothing but God,

Or mediate or direct,

Nothing but God,

The Husband of the Heavens :

And who Him love, in potence great or small,

Are, one and all,

Heirs of the Palace glad

And inly clad

With the bridal robes of ardour virginal.

XXIX.

DEAD LANGUAGE.

" THOU dost not wisely, Bard.

A double voice is Truth's, to use at will:

One, with the abysmal scorn of good for ill,

Smiting the brutish ear with doctrine hard,

Wherein She strives to look as near a lie

As can comport with her divinity ;

The other tender-soft as seem

The embraces of a dead Love in a dream.

These thoughts, which you have sung

In the vernacular,

Should be, as others of the Church's are,

Decently cloak'd in the Imperial Tongue.

Have you no fears

Lest, as Lord Jesus bids your sort to dread,

Yon acorn-munchers rend you limb from limb,

You, with Heaven's liberty affronting theirs!"

So spoke my monitor; but I to him,

" Alas, and is not mine a language dead?"

XXX.

1867.

In the year of the great crime,

When the false English Nobles and their Jew,

By God demented, slew

The Trust they stood twice pledged to keep from wrong,

One said, Take up thy Song,

That breathes the mild and almost mythic time

Of England's prime!

But I, Ah, me,

The freedom of the few

That, in our free Land, were indeed the free,

Can song renew ?

Ill singing 'tis with blotting prison-bars,

How high soe'er, betwixt us and the stars ;

Ill singing 'tis when there are none to hear ;

And days are near

When England shall forget

The fading glow which, for a little while,

Illumes her yet,

The lovely smile

That grows so faint and wan,

Her people shouting in her dying ear,

Are not daws twain worth two of any swan !

   Ye outlaw'd Best, who yet are bright

With the sunken light,

Whose common style

Is Virtue at her gracious ease,

The flower of olden sanctities,

Ye haply trust, by love's benignant guile,

To lure the dark and selfish brood

To their own hated good;

Ye haply dream

Your lives shall still their charmful sway sustain,

Unstifled by the fever'd steam

That rises from the plain.

Know, 'twas the force of function high,

In corporate exercise, and public awe

Of Nature's, Heaven's, and England's Law

That Best, though mix'd with Bad, should reign,

Which kept you in your sky!

But, when the sordid Trader caught

The loose-held sceptre from your hands distraught,

And soon, to the Mechanic vain,

Sold the proud toy for nought,

Your charm was broke, your task was sped,

Your beauty, with your honour, dead,

And though you still are dreaming sweet

Of being even now not less

Than Gods and Goddesses, ye shall not long so cheat

Your hearts of their due heaviness.

Go, get you for your evil watching shriven!

Leave to your lawful Master's itching hands

Your unking'd lands,

But keep, at least, the dignity

Of deigning not, for his smooth use, to be,

Voteless, the voted delegates

Of his strange interests, loves and hates.

In sackcloth, or in private strife

With private ill, ye may please Heaven,

And soothe the coming pangs of sinking life;

And prayer perchance may win

A term to God's indignant mood

And the orgies of the multitude,—

Which now begin;

But do not hope to wave the silken rag

Of your unsanction'd flag,

And so to guide

The great ship, helmless on the swelling tide

Of that presumptuous Sea,

Unlit by sun or moon, yet inly bright

With lights innumerable that give no light,

Flames of corrupted will and scorn of right

Rejoicing to be free.

 And now, because the dark comes on apace

When none can work for fear,

And Liberty in every Land lies slain,

And the two Tyrannies unchallenged reign,

And heavy prophecies, suspended long

At supplication of the righteous few

And so discredited, to fulfilment throng

Restrain'd no more by faithful prayer or tear,

And the dread baptism of blood seems near

That brings to the humbled Earth the Time of Grace,

Hush'd be all song,

And let Christ's own look through

The darkness, suddenly increased,

To the grey secret lingering in the East.

XXXI.

VESICA PISCIS.

In strenuous hope I wrought,

And hope seem'd still betray'd;

Lastly I said,

"I have labour'd through the Night, nor yet

" Have taken aught;

" But at Thy word I will again cast forth the net!"

And, lo, I caught

(Oh, quite unlike and quite beyond my thought,)

Not the quick, shining harvest of the Sea,

For food, my wish,

But Thee

Then, hiding even in me,

As hid was Simon's coin within the fish,

Thou sigh'd'st, with joy, " Be dumb,

" Or speak but of forgotten things to far-off times

    to come."

XXXII.

SING US ONE OF THE SONGS OF SION.

How sing the Lord's Song in so strange a Land?
A torrid waste of water-mocking sand;
Oases of wild grapes;
A dull, malodorous fog
O'er a once Sacred River's wandering strand,
Its ancient tillage all gone back to bog;
A busy synod of blest cats and apes
Exposing the poor trick of earth and star
With worshipp'd snouts oracular;

Prophets to whose blind stare

The heavens the glory of God do not declare,

Skill'd in such question nice

As why one conjures toads who fails with lice,

And hatching snakes from sticks in such a swarm

As quite to surfeit Aaron's bigger worm ;

A nation which has got

A lie in her right hand,

And knows it not;

With Pharaohs to her mind, each drifting as a log

Which way the foul stream flows,

More harden'd the more plagued with fly and frog !

How should sad Exile sing in such a Land ?

How should ye understand ?

What could he win but jeers,

Or howls, such as sweet music draws from dog,

Who told of marriage-feasting to the man

That nothing knows of food but bread of bran ?

Besides, if aught such ears

Might e'er unclog,

There lives but one,

(Hear not this praise, meek walls of Edgbaston !)

With tones for Sion meet.

Behoveful, zealous, beautiful, elect,

Mild, firm, judicious, loving, bold, discreet,

Without superfluousness, without defect,

Few are his words, and find but scant respect,

Nay, scorn from some, for God's good cause agog.

Silence in such a Land is oftenest such men's speech.

O, that I might his holy secret reach ;

O, might I catch his mantle when he goes ;

O, that I were so gentle and so sweet,

So I might deal fair Sion's foolish foes

Such blows !

K

XXXIII.

EROS AND PSYCHE.

"Love, I heard tell of thee so oft!
Yea, thrice my face and bosom flush'd with heat
Of sudden wings,
Through delicatest ether feathering soft
Their solitary beat.
Long did I muse what service or what charms
Might lure thee, blissful Bird, into mine arms;
And nets I made,

But not of the fit strings.

At last, of endless failure much afraid,

To-night I would do nothing but lie still,

And promise, wert thou once within my window-sill,

Thine unknown will.

In nets' default,

Finch-like meseem'd thou might'st be ta'en with salt ;

And here—and how thou mad'st me start !—

Thou art."

  "O Mortal, by Immortals' cunning led,

Who shew'd thee how for Gods to bait thy bed ?

Ah, Psyche, guess'd you nought

I craved but to be caught?

Wanton, it was not you,

But I that did so passionately sue ;

And for your beauty, not unscath'd, I fought

With Hades, ere I own'd in you a thought !"

  "O, heavenly Lover true,

Is this your mouth upon my forehead press'd ?

Are these your arms about my bosom link'd ?

Are these your hands that tremble near my heart,

Where join two hearts, for juncture more distinct ?

By thee and by my maiden zone caress'd,

What dim, waste tracts of life shine sudden, like moonbeams

On windless ocean, shaken by sweet dreams !

Ah, stir not to depart !

Kiss me again, your Wife and Virgin too !

O Love, that, like a rose,

Deckest my breast with beautiful repose,

Kiss me again, and clasp me round the heart,

Till fill'd with thee am I

As the cocoon is with the butterfly !

—Yet how 'scape quite

Nor pluck pure pleasure with profane delight ?

How know I that my Love is what he seems !

Give me a sign

That, in the pitchy night,

Comes to my pillow an immortal Spouse,

And not a fiend, hiding with happy boughs

Of palm and asphodel

The pits of hell!"

 " 'Tis this :

I make the childless to keep joyful house.

Below thy bosom, mortal Mistress mine,

Immortal by my kiss,

Leaps what sweet pain ?

A fiend, my Psyche, comes with barren bliss,

A God's embraces never are in vain."

 " I own

A life not mine within my golden zone.

Yea, how

'Tis easier grown

Thine arduous rule to don

Than for a Bride to put her bride-dress on !

Nay, rather, now

'Tis no more service to be borne serene,

Whither thou wilt, thy stormful wings between.

But, Oh,

Can I endure

This flame, yet live for what thou lov'st me, pure?"

" Himself the God let blame

If all about him bursts to quenchless flame !

My Darling, know

Thy spotless fairness is not match'd in snow,

But in the integrity of fire.

Whate'er thou art, Sweet, I require.

A sorry God were he

That fewer claim'd than all Love's mighty kingdoms

    three !"

" Much marvel I

That thou, the greatest of the Powers above,

Me visitest with such exceeding love.

What thing is this?

A God to make me, nothing, needful to his bliss,

And humbly wait my favour for a kiss!

Yea, all thy legions of liege deity

To look into this mystery desire."

" Content thee, Dear, with them, this marvel to admire,

And lay thy foolish little head to rest

On my familiar breast.

Should a high King, leaving his arduous throne,

Sue from her hedge a little Gipsy Maid,

For far-off royal ancestry bewray'd

By some wild beauties, to herself unknown;

Some voidness of herself in her strange ways

Which to his bounteous fulness promised dainty praise;

Some power, by all but him unguess'd,

Of growing king-like were she king-caress'd;

And should he bid his dames of loftiest grade

Put off her rags and make her lowlihead

Pure for the soft midst of his perfumed bed,

So to forget, kind-couch'd with her alone,

His empire, in her winsome joyance free ;

What would he do, if such a fool were she

As at his grandeur there to gape and quake,

Mindless of love's supreme equality,

And of his heart, so simple for her sake

That all he ask'd, for making her all-blest,

Was that her nothingness alway

Should yield such easy fee as frank to play

Or sleep delighted in her Monarch's breast,

Feeling her nothingness her giddiest boast,

As being the charm for which he loved her most ?

What if this reed,

Through which the King thought love-tunes to have blown,

Should shriek, ' Indeed,

' I am too base to trill so blest a tone !'

Would not the King allege

Defaulted consummation of the marriage-pledge,

And hie the Gipsy to her native hedge?"

"O, too much joy; O, touch of airy fire;

O, turmoil of content; O, unperturb'd desire,

From founts of spirit impell'd through brain and blood!

I'll not call ill what, since 'tis thine, is good,

Nor best what is but second best or third;

Still my heart fails,

And, unaccustom'd and astonished, quails,

And blames me, though I think I have not err'd.

'Tis hard for fly, in such a honied flood,

To use his eyes, far less his wings or feet.

Bitter be thy behests!

Lie like a bunch of myrrh between my aching breasts.

Some greatly pangful penance would I brave.

Sharpness me save

From being slain by sweet!"

"In thy dell'd bosom's double peace

Let all care cease!

Custom's joy-killing breath

Shall bid thee sue full soon for custom-killing death.

So clasp thy childish arms again around my heart :

'Tis but in such captivity

The unbounded Heav'ns know what they be !

And lie thou there,

Till the dawn, threat'ning to declare

My beauty, which thou canst not bear,

Bid me depart.

Suffer thy soul's delight,

Lest that which is to come wither thee quite :

For these are only thine espousals ; yes,

More intimate and fruitfuller far

Than aptest mortal nuptials are ;

But nuptials wait thee such as now thou darest not guess."

　　"In all I thee obey !　And thus I know

That all is well :

Should'st thou me tell

Out of thy warm caress to go

And roll my body in the biting snow,

My very body's joy were but increased ;

More pleasant 'tis to please thee than be pleased.

Thy love has conquer'd me; do with me as thou wilt,

And use me as a chattel that is thine !

Kiss, tread me under foot, cherish or beat,

Sheathe in my heart sharp pain up to the hilt,

Invent what else were most perversely sweet ;

Nay, let the Fiend drag me through dens of guilt;

Let Earth, Heav'n, Hell

'Gainst my content combine ;

What could make nought the touch that made thee mine !

Ah, say not yet, farewell !"

   "Nay, that's the Blackbird's note, the sweet Night's

      knell.

Behold, Belov'd, the penance thou would'st brave !"

" Curs'd, when it comes, the bitter thing we crave !

Thou leav'st me now, like to the moon at dawn,

A little, vacuous world alone in air.

I will not care !

When dark comes back my dark shall be withdrawn !

Go free ;

For 'tis with me

As when the cup the Child scoops in the sand

Fills, and is part and parcel of the Sea.

I'll say it to myself and understand.

Farewell !

Go as thou wilt and come !   Lover divine,

Thou still art jealously and wholly mine;

And this thy kiss

A separate secret by none other scann'd;

Though well I wis

The whole of life is womanhood to thee,

Momently wedded with enormous bliss.

Rainbow, that hast my heaven sudden spann'd,

I am the apple of thy glorious gaze,

Each else life cent'ring to a different blaze;

And, nothing though I be

But now a no more void capacity for thee,

'Tis all to know there's not in air or land

Another for thy Darling quite like me!

Mine arms no more thy restless plumes compel!

Farewell!

Whilst thou art gone, I'll search the weary meads

To deck my bed with lilies of fair deeds!

And, if thou choose to come this eventide,

A touch, my Love, will set my casement wide.

Farewell, farewell!

Be my dull days

Music, at least, with thy remember'd praise!"

"Bitter, sweet, few and veil'd let be

Thy songs of me.

205   Preserving bitter, very sweet,

Few, that so all may be discreet,

And veil'd, that, seeing, none may see."

XXXIV.

THE CRY AT MIDNIGHT.

THE Midge's wing beats to and fro
A thousand times ere one can utter "O!"
And Sirius' ball
Does on his business run
As many times immenser than the Sun.
Why should things not be great as well as small,
Or move like light as well as move at all?
St. Michael fills his place, I mine, and, if you please,

We will respect each other's provinces,

I marv'lling not at him, nor he at me.

But, if thou must go gaping, let it be

That One who could make Michael should make thee.

O, foolish Man, meting things low and high

By self, that accidental quantity!

With this conceit, Philosophy stalks frail

As peacock staggering underneath his tail.

Who judge of Plays from their own penny gaff,

At God's great theatre will hiss and laugh;

For what's a Saint to them

Brought up in modern virtues brummagem?

With garments grimed and lamps gone all to snuff,

And counting others for like Virgins queer,

To list those others cry, " Our Bridegroom's near!"

Meaning their God, is surely quite enough

To make them rend their clothes and bawl out

    " Blasphemy!"

XXXV.

DE NATURA DEORUM.

" GOOD-MORROW, Psyche !   What's thine errand now ?
What awful pleasure do thine eyes bespeak,
What shame is in thy baby cheek,
What terror on thy brow ?
Is this my Psyche, once so pale and meek ?
Thy body's sudden beauty my sight old
Stings, like an agile bead of boiling gold,
And all thy life looks troubled like a tree's

Whose boughs wave many ways in one great breeze."

"O Pythoness, to strangest story hark :

A dreadful God was with me in the dark—"

"How many a Maid—

Has never told me that! And thou'rt afraid—"

"He'll come no more,

Or-come but twice,

Or thrice,

Or only thrice ten thousand times thrice o'er !"

"For want of wishing thou mean'st not to miss.

We know the Lover, Psyche, by the kiss !"

"If speech of honey could impart the sweet,

The world were all in tears and at his feet !

But not to tell of that in tears come I, but this :

I'm foolish, weak, and small,

And fear to fall.

If long he stay away, O, frightful dream, wise Mother,

What keeps me but that I, gone crazy, kiss some other !"

" The fault were his !   But, know,

Sweet little Daughter sad,

He did but feign to go,

And never more

Shall cross thy window-sill,

Or pass beyond thy door,

Save by thy will.

He's present now in some dim place apart

Of the ivory house wherewith thou mad'st him glad.

Nay, this I whisper thee,

Since none is near,

Or, if one were, since only thou could'st hear,

That happy thing which makes thee flush and start, —

Like infant lips in contact with thy heart,

Is He !"

" Yea, this I know, but never can believe !

O, hateful light ! when shall mine own eyes mark

My beauty, which this victory did achieve ?"

" When thou, like Gods and owls, canst see by dark."

" In vain I cleanse me from all blurring error—"

" 'Tis the last rub that polishes the mirror."

" It takes fresh blurr each breath which I respire."

" Poor Child, don't cry so !   Hold it to the fire."

" Ah, nought these dints can e'er do out again !"

" Love is not love which does not sweeter live

For having something dreadful to forgive."

" Sadness and change and pain

Shall me for ever stain ;

For, though my blissful fate

Be for a billion years,

How shall I stop my tears

That life was once so low and Love arrived so late !"

" Sadness is beauty's savour, and pain is

The exceedingly keen edge of bliss,

Nor, without swift mutation, would the heav'ns be aught."

" How to behave with him I'd fain be taught.

A Maid, meseems, within a God's embrace,

Should bear her like a Goddess, or, at least, a Grace."

  " When Gods, to Man or Maid below,

As men or birds appear,

A kind 'tis of incognito,

And that, not them, is what they choose we should revere."

  " Advise me what oblation vast to bring,

Some least part of my worship to confess !"

  " A woman is a little thing,

And in things little lies her comeliness."

  " Must he not soon with mortal tire to toy ?"

  " The bashful meeting of strange Depth and Height

Breeds the forever new-born babe, Delight;

And, as thy God is more than mortal boy,

So bashful more the meeting, and so more the joy."

  " He loves me dearly, but he shakes a whip

Of deathless scorpions at my slightest slip.

Mother, last night he call'd me 'Gipsy,' so

Roughly it smote me like a blow !

Yet, oh,

I love him, as none surely e'er could love

Our People's pompous but good-natured Jove.

He used to send me stately overture ;

But marriage-bonds, till now, I never could endure !"

  " How should great Jove himself do else than miss

To win the woman he forgets to kiss ;

Or, won, to keep his favour in her eyes,

If he's too soft or sleepy to chastise !

By Eros, her twain claims are ne'er forgot ;

Her wedlock's marr'd when either's miss'd :

Or when she's kiss'd, but beaten not,

Or duly beaten, but not kiss'd.

Ah, Child, the sweet

Content, when we're both kiss'd and beat !

—But whence these wounds?   What Demon thee enjoins

To scourge thy shoulders white

And tender loins !"

" 'Tis nothing, Mother.   Happiness at play,

And speech of tenderness no speech can say !"

" How learn'd thou art !   .

Twelve honeymoons profane had taught thy docile heart

Less than thine Eros, in a summer night !"

" Nay, do not jeer, but help my puzzled plight :

Because he loves so marvellously me,

And I with all he loves in love must be,

How to except myself I do not see.

Yea, now that other vanities are vain,

I'm vain, since him it likes, of being withal

Weak, foolish, small !"

" How can a Maid forget her ornaments !

The Powers, that hopeless doom the proud to die,

Unask'd smile pardon upon vanity,

Nay, praise it, when themselves are praised thereby."

" Ill-match'd I am for a God's blandishments !

So great, so wise—"

"Gods, in the abstract, are, no doubt, most wise ;

But, in the concrete, well, they're mysteries !

He's not with thee,

At all less wise nor more

Than human Lover is with her he deigns to adore.

He finds a fair capacity,

And fills it with himself, and glad would die

For that sole She."

"Know'st thou some potion me awake to keep,

Lest, to the grief of that ne'er-slumbering Bliss,

Disgraced I sleep,

Wearied in soul by his bewildering kiss ?"

"The Immortals, Psyche, moulded men from sods

That Maids from them might learn the ways of Gods.

Think, would a wakeful Youth his hard fate weep,

Lock'd to the tired breast of a Bride asleep ?"

"Ah, me, I do not dream,

Yet all this does some heathen fable seem !"

"O'ermuch thou mind'st the throne he leaves above !

Between unequals sweet is equal love."

"Nay, Mother, in his breast, when darkness blinds,

I cannot for my life but talk and laugh

With the large impudence of little minds !"

"Respectful to the Gods and meek,

According to one's lights, I grant

'Twere well to be ;

But, on my word,

Child, any one, to hear you speak,

Would take you for a Protestant,

(Such fish I do foresee

When the charm'd fume comes strong on me,)

Or powder'd lackey, by some great man's board,

A deal more solemn than his Lord !

Know'st thou not, Girl, thine Eros loves to laugh ?

And shall a God do anything by half ?

He foreknew and predestinated all

The Great must pay for kissing things so small,

And ever loves his little Maid the more

The more she makes him laugh."

  " O, Mother, are you sure?"

  " Gaze steady where yon starless deep the gaze revolts,

And say,

Seest thou a Titan forging thunderbolts,

Or three fair butterflies at lovesome play?

And this I'll add, for succour of thy soul :

Lines parallel meet sooner than some think ;

The least part oft is greater than the whole ;

And, when you're thirsty, that's the time to drink."

  " Thy sacred words I ponder and revere,

And thank thee heartily that some are clear."

  " Clear speech to men is mostly speech in vain.

Their wit is by themselves so justly scann'd,

They still despise the things they understand ;

But, to a pretty Maid like thee, I don't mind speaking

    plain."

    " Then one boon more to her whom strange Fate mocks

With a wife's duty but no wife's sweet right :

Could I at will but summon my Delight—"

    " Thou of thy Jewel art the dainty box ;

Thine is the charm which, any time, unlocks ;

And this, it seems, thou hitt'st upon last night.

Now go, Child !   For thy sake

I've talk'd till this stiff tripod makes my old limbs ache."

XXXVI.

WINTER.

I, SINGULARLY moved

To love the lovely that are not beloved,

Of all the Seasons, most

Love Winter, and to trace

The sense of the Trophonian pallor on her face.

It is not death, but plenitude of peace;

And the dim cloud that does the world enfold

Hath less the characters of dark and cold

Than warmth and light asleep;

And correspondent breathing seems to keep

With the infant harvest, breathing soft below

Its eider coverlet of snow.

Nor is in field or garden anything

But, duly look'd into, contains serene

The substance of things hoped for, in the Spring,

And evidence of Summer not yet seen.

On every chance-mild day

That visits the moist shaw,

The honeysuckle, 'sdaining to be crost

In urgence of sweet life by sleet or frost,

'Voids the time's law

With still increase

Of leaflet new, and little, wandering spray;

Often, in sheltering brakes,

As one from rest disturb'd in the first hour,

Primrose or violet bewilder'd wakes,

And deems 'tis time to flower;

Though not a whisper of her voice he hear,

The buried bulb does know

The signals of the year,

And hails far Summer with his lifted spear;

The gorse-field dark, by sudden, gold caprice,

Turns, here and there, into a Jason's fleece;

Lilies that, soon in Autumn, slipp'd their gowns of green

And vanish'd into earth,

And came again, ere Autumn died, to birth,

Stand full-array'd amidst the wavering shower,

And perfect for the Summer, less the flower;

In nook of pale or crevice of crude bark,

Thou canst not miss,

If close thou spy, to mark

The ghostly chrysalis,

That, if thou touch it, stirs in its dream dark;

And the flush'd Robin, in the evenings hoar,

Does of Love's Day, as if he saw it, sing;

But sweeter yet than dream or song of Summer or Spring

Are Winter's sometime smiles, that seem to well

From infancy ineffable;

Her wandering, languorous gaze,

So unfamiliar, so without amaze,

On the elemental, chill adversity,

The uncomprehended rudeness; and her sigh

And solemn, gathering tear,

And look of exile from some great repose, the sphere

Of ether, moved by ether only, or

By something still more tranquil.—

XXXVII.

PSYCHE'S DISCONTENT.

" Not yet, not yet !

'Tis still high day, and half my toil's to do.

How can I toil, if thus thou dost renew

Toil's guerdon, which the daytime should forget ?

The long, long night, when none can work for fear,

Sweet fear incessantly consummated,

My most divinely Dear,

My Joy, my Dread,

Will soon be here !

Not, Eros, yet !

I ask, for Day, the use which is the Wife's :

To bear, apart from thy delight and thee,

The fardel coarse of customary life's

Exceeding injucundity.

Leave me awhile, that I may shew thee clear

How Goddess-like thy love has lifted me ;

How, seeming lone upon the gaunt, lone shore,

I'll trust thee near,

When thou'rt, to knowledge of my heart, no more

Than a dream's heed

Of lost joy track'd in scent of the sea-weed !

Leave me to pluck the incomparable flower

Of frailty lion-like fighting in thy name and power ;

To make thee laugh, in thy safe heaven, to see

With what grip fell

I'll cling to hope when life draws hard to hell,

M

Yea, cleave to thee when me thou seem'st to slay,

Haply, at close of some most cruel day,

To find myself in thy reveal'd arms clasp'd,

Just when I say,

My feet have slipp'd at last !

But, lo, while thus I store toil's slow increase,

To be my dower, in patience and in peace,

Thou com'st, like bolt from blue, invisibly,

With premonition none nor any sign,

And, at a gasp, no choice nor fault of mine,

Possess'd I am with thee

Ev'n as a sponge is by a surge of the sea !"

   " Thus irresistibly by Love embraced

Is she who boasts her more than mortal chaste !"

   " Count'st thou me worthy, then, by day and night,

But of this fond indignity, delight?"

   " Little, bold Feminility,

That darest blame Heaven, what would'st thou have or be?"

" Shall I, the gnat which dances in thy ray,

Dare to be reverent?   Therefore dare I say,

I cannot guess the good that I desire,

But this I know, I spurn the gifts which Hell

Can mock till which is which 'tis hard to tell.

I love thee, God; yea, and 'twas such assault

As this which made me thine ; if that be fault;

But I, thy Mistress, merit should thine ire

If aught so little, transitory and low

As this which made me thine

Should hold me so."

 " Little to thee, my Psyche, is this, but much to me !"

 " Ah, if, my God, that be !"

 " Yea, Palate fine,

That claim'st for thy proud cup the pearl of price,

And scorn'st the wine,

Accept the sweet, and say 'tis sacrifice !

Sleep, Centre to the tempest of my love,

M 2

And dream thereof,

And keep the smile which sleeps within thy face

Like sunny eve in some forgotten place !"

"Enough, enough, ambrosial plumed Boy !

My bosom is aweary of thy breath.

Thou kissest joy

To death.

Have pity of my clay-conceived birth

And maiden's simple mood,

Which longs for ether and infinitude,

As thou, being God, crav'st littleness and earth !

Thou art immortal, thou canst ever toy,

Nor savour less

The sweets of thine eternal childishness,

And hold thy godhead bright in far employ.

Me, to quite other custom life-inured,

Ah, loose from thy caress.

'Tis not to be endured !

Undo thine arms and let me see the sky,

By this infatuating flame obscured.

O, I should feel thee nearer to my heart

If thou and I

Shone each to each respondently apart,

Like stars which one the other trembling spy,

Distinct and lucid in extremes of air.

O, hear me pray——"

   " Be prudent in thy prayer !

A God is bond to her who is wholly his,

And may not her beseeched harm deny."

   " Nay, hear me not amiss.

I could not mean that thou should'st ne'er me kiss ;

But, since thou count'st me all too mean to share

The sorrows of a God, which are, as well

As his felicities, ineffable,

Ah, let these accidents of love go by,

These eddies of thy bliss ;

Let them rush by,

And leave i' the flood some turfy islet calm,

Where we two, all the day,

May sing without annoy

Under the fragrant bay

Or fanning palm ;

Or nurse the sigh-reciprocated joy

Of incommunicable moods

With lonesome odours of the lonely woods ;

Or watch, in star-sweet dark, the boreal chase,

The electric, swift desire,

Making glad conquest of obstructing space

In streams of bashful light and free, ethereal fire,

With 'twixt us peace, like peace of Babe and Mother,

One Innocency feeding from itself the other."

XXXVIII.

ARBOR VITÆ.

With honeysuckle, over-sweet, festoon'd ;

With bitter ivy bound ;

Terraced with funguses unsound ;

Deform'd with many a boss

And closed scar, o'ercushion'd deep with moss ;

Bunch'd all about with pagan mistletoe ;

And thick with nests of the hoarse bird

That talks, but understands not his own word ;

Stands, and so stood a thousand years ago,

A single tree.

Thunder has done its worst among its twigs,

Where the great crest yet blackens, never pruned,

But in its heart, alway

Ready to push new verdurous boughs, whene'er

The rotting saplings near it fall and leave it air,

Is all antiquity and no decay.

Rich, though rejected by the forest-pigs,

Its fruit, beneath whose rough, concealing rind

They that will break it find

Heart-succouring savour of each several meat,

And kernell'd drink of brain-renewing power,

With bitter condiment and sour,

And sweet economy of sweet,

And odours that remind

Of haunts of childhood and a different day.

Beside this tree,

Praising no Gods nor blaming, sans a wish,

Sits, Tartar-like, the Time's civility,

And eats its dead-dog off a golden dish.

XXXIX.

SPONSA DEI.

WHAT is this Maiden fair

The laughing of whose eye

Is in man's heart renew'd virginity;

Who yet sick longing breeds

For marriage which exceeds

The inventive guess of Love to satisfy

With hope of utter binding, and of loosing endless

    dear despair?

What gleams about her shine,

More transient than delight and more divine!

If she does something but a little sweet,

As gaze towards the glass to set her hair,

See how his soul falls humbled at her feet!

Her gentle step, to go or come,

Gains her more merit than a martyrdom;

And, if she dance, it doth such grace confer

As opes the heaven of heavens to more than her,

And makes a rival of her worshipper.

To die unknown for her were little cost!

So is she without guile,

Her mere refusèd smile

Makes up the sum of that which may be lost!

Who is this Fair

Whom each hath seen,

The darkest once in this bewailed dell,

Be he not destin'd for the glooms of hell?

Whom each hath seen

And known, with sharp remorse and sweet, as Queen

And tear-glad Mistress of his hopes of bliss,

Too fair for man to kiss?

Who is this only happy She,

Whom, by a frantic flight of courtesy,

Born of despair

Of better lodging for his Spirit fair,

He adores as Margaret, Maude, or Cecily?

And what this sigh,

That each one heaves for earth's last lowlihead

And the Heaven high

Ineffably lock'd in dateless bridal-bed?

Are all, then, mad, or is it prophecy?

" Sons now we are of God," as we have heard,

" But what we shall be hath not yet appear'd."

O, Heart, remember thee

That Man is none,

Save One.

What if this Lady be thyself, and He

Who claims to enjoy her sacred beauty be,

Not thou, but God; and thy sick fire

A female vanity,

Such as a Bride, viewing her mirror'd charms,

Feels when she sighs, "All these are for his arms!"

A reflex heat

Flash'd on thy cheek from His immense desire,

Which waits to crown, beyond thy brain's conceit,

Thy nameless, secret, hopeless longing sweet,

Not by-and-bye, but now,

Unless deny Him thou!

XL.

TO THE BODY.

CREATION's and Creator's crowning good;

Wall of infinitude;

Foundation of the sky,

In Heaven forecast

And long'd for from eternity,

Though laid the last;

Reverberating dome,

Of music cunningly built home

Against the void and indolent disgrace

Of unresponsive space;

Little, sequester'd pleasure-house

For God and for his Spouse;

Elaborately, yea, past conceiving, fair,

Since, from the graced decorum of the hair,

Ev'n to the tingling, sweet

Soles of the simple, earth-confiding feet,

And from the inmost heart

Outwards unto the thin

Silk curtains of the skin,

Every least part

Astonish'd hears

And sweet replies to some like region of the spheres;

Form'd for a dignity prophets but darkly name,

Lest shameless men cry " Shame !"

So rich with wealth conceal'd

That Heaven and Hell fight chiefly for this field;

Clinging to everything that pleases thee

With indefectible fidelity;

Alas, so true

To all thy friendships that no grace

Thee from thy sin can wholly disembrace;

Which thus 'bides with thee as the Jebusite,

That, maugre all God's promises could do,

The chosen People never conquer'd quite;

Who therefore lived with them,

And that by formal truce and as of right,

In metropolitan Jerusalem.

For which false fealty

Thou needs must, for a season, lie

In the grave's arms, foul and unshriven,

Albeit, in Heaven,

Thy crimson-throbbing Glow

Into its old abode aye pants to go,

And does with envy sce

Enoch, Elijah, and the Lady, she

Who left the lilies in her body's lieu.

O, if the pleasures I have known in thee

But my poor faith's poor first-fruits be,

What quintessential, keen, ethereal bliss

Then shall be his

Who has thy birth-time's consecrating dew

For death's sweet chrism retain'd,

Quick, tender, virginal, and unprofaned !

XLI.

AURAS OF DELIGHT.

BEAUTIFUL habitations, auras of delight!

Who shall bewail the crags and bitter foam

And angry sword-blades flashing left and right

Which guard your glittering height,

That none thereby may come!

The vision which we have

Revere we so,

That yet we crave

To foot those fields of ne'er-profanèd snow ?

  I, with heart-quake,

Dreaming or thinking of that realm of Love,

See, oft, a dove

Tangled in frightful nuptials with a snake,

The tortured knot,

Now, like a kite scant-weighted, flung bewitch'd

Sunwards, now pitch'd,

Tail over head, down, but with no taste got

Eternally

Of rest in either ruin or the sky,

But bird and vermin each incessant strives,

With vain dilaceration of both lives,

'Gainst its abhorred bond insoluble,

Coveting fiercer any separate hell

Than the most weary Soul in Purgatory

On God's sweet breast to lie.

  And, in this sign, I con

The guerdon of that golden Cup, fulfill'd

With fornications foul of Babylon,

The heart where good is well-perceiv'd and known,

Yet is not will'd ;

And Him I thank, who can make live again

The dust, but not the joy we once profane,

That I, of ye,

Beautiful habitations, auras of delight,

In childish years, and since had sometime sense and sight,

But that ye vanish'd quite,

Even from memory,

Ere I could get my breath, and whisper " See !"

 But did for me

They altogether die,

Those trackless glories glimps'd in upper sky ?

Were they of chance, or vain,

Nor good at all again

For curb of heart or fret ?

Nay, though, by grace,

Lest, haply, I refuse God to his face,

Their likeness wholly I forget,

Ah, yet,

Often in straits which else for me were ill,

I mind me still

I *did* respire the lonely auras sweet,

I *did* the blest abodes behold, and, at the mountains' feet,

Bathed in the holy Stream by Hermon's thymy hill.

XLII.

THE AZALEA.

THERE, where the sun shines first

Against our room,

She train'd the gold Azalea, whose perfume

She, Spring-like, from her breathing grace dispersed.

Last night the delicate crests of saffron bloom,

For that their dainty likeness watch'd and nurst,

Were just at point to burst.

At dawn I dream'd, O God, that she was dead,

And groan'd aloud upon my wretched bed,

And waked, ah, God, and did not waken her,

But lay, with eyes still closed,

Perfectly bless'd in the delicious sphere

By which I knew so well that she was near,

My heart to speechless thankfulness composed.

Till 'gan to stir

A dizzy somewhat in my troubled head—

It *was* the azalea's breath, and she *was* dead !

The warm night had the lingering buds disclosed ;

And I had fall'n asleep with to my breast

A chance-found letter press'd

In which she said,

" So, till to-morrow eve, my Own, adieu !

" Parting's well-paid with soon again to meet,

" Soon in your arms to feel so small and sweet,

" Sweet to myself that am so sweet to you !"

XLIII.

SAINT VALENTINE'S DAY.

WELL dost thou, Love, thy solemn Feast to hold
In vestal February,
Not rather choosing out some rosy day
From the rich coronet of the coming May,
When all things meet to marry!
  O, quick, prævernal Power
That signall'st punctual through the sleepy mould
The Snowdrop's time to flower

Fair as the rash oath of virginity

Which is first-love's first cry;

O, Baby Spring,

That flutter'st sudden 'neath the breast of Earth

A month before the birth;

Whence is the peaceful poignancy,

The joy contrite,

Sadder than sorrow, sweeter than delight,

That burthens now the breath of everything,

Though each one sighs as if to each alone

The cherish'd pang were known?

At dusk of dawn, on his dark spray apart,

With it the Blackbird breaks the young Day's heart;

In evening's hush

About it talks the heavenly-minded Thrush;

The hill with like remorse

Smiles to the Sun's smile in his westering course;

The fisher's drooping skiff

In yonder sheltering bay;

The choughs that call about the shining cliff;

The children, noisy in the setting ray,

Own the sweet season, each thing as it may;

Thoughts of strange kindness and forgotten peace

In me increase;

And tears arise

Within my happy, happy Mistress' eyes,

And, lo, her lips, averted from my kiss,

Ask from Love's bounty much, much more than bliss.

   Is't the sequester'd and exceeding sweet

Of dear Desire electing his defeat?

Is't the waked Earth now to yon purpling cope

Uttering first-love's first cry,

Vainly renouncing, with a Seraph's sigh,

Love's natural hope?

Fair-meaning Earth, foredoom'd to perjury!

Behold, all-amorous May,

With roses heap'd upon her laughing brows,

Avoids thee of thy vows!

Were it for thee, with her warm bosom near,

To abide the sharpness of the Seraph's sphere?

Forget thy foolish words;

Go to her summons gay,

Thy heart with dead, wing'd Innocencies fill'd,

Ev'n as a nest with birds

After the old ones by the hawk are kill'd.

  Well dost thou, Love, to celebrate

The noon of thy soft ecstasy

Or e'er it be too late,

Or e'er the Snowdrop die!

XLIV.

ALEXANDER AND LYCON.

" What, no crown won,

These two whole years,

By man of fortitude beyond his peers,

In Thrace or Macedon ?"

" No, none.

But what deep trouble does my Lycon feel,

And hide 'neath chat about the commonweal ?"

" Glaucé but now the third time did again

The thing which I forbade.   I had to box her ears.

'Twas ill to see her both blue eyes

Settled in tears

Despairing on the skies,

And the poor lip all pucker'd into pain ;

Yet, for her sake, from kisses to refrain !"

　" Ho, Timocles, take down

That crown.

No, not that common one for blood with extreme valour

　　spilt,

But yonder, with the berries gilt.

'Tis, Lycon, thy just meed.

To inflict unmoved

And firm to bear the woes of the Beloved

Is fortitude indeed."

XLV.

THE MERRY MURDER.

STAND by,

Ye Wise, by whom Heav'n rules!

Your kingly hands suit not the hangman's tools.

When God has doom'd a glorious Past to die,

Are there no knaves and fools?

Content ye for a space to count for nought.

Smoke of the strife of other Powers

Than ours

And tongues inscrutable with fury fraught

'Wilder the sky,

Till the new thing we know not how to ask be wrought.

Stand by !

Since tears are vain, here let us look and laugh,

But not too loudly ; for the brave time's come,

The establish'd sanctity of slop and slum,

When Best may not blaspheme the Bigger Half,

And freedom for our sort means freedom to be dumb.

   Lo, how the dross and draff

Grin up at us, and shout,

" The Morning's ours, the Night is theirs !"

And urge their rout

Where the wild dawn of rising Tartarus flares.

Yon strives a Leader, lusting to be seen.

His leprosy's so perfect that men call him clean !

Listen the long, sincere, and liberal bray

Of the earnest Puller at another's hay

'Gainst aught that dares to tug the other way,

Quite void of fears

With all that noise of ruin round his ears!

There goes another of a different feather;

But, where two rogues are, two still run together;

And the fresh Dame, whose pleasures they purvey,

Though shock'd by Turk, likes reasonable range,

Chadband her choice, with Chiffinch for a change!

Yonder a prophet casts his cap o'erhead,

And swears the threaten'd doom is ne'er to dread

That's come, though not yet past.

All front the horror and are none aghast;

Brag of their full-blown rights and liberties,

Nor once surmise

When each man gets his due the Nation dies;

Nay, still shout "Progress!" as if seven plagues

Should take the man who stopp'd to stretch his legs.

    At last, indeed,

We, too, can bid the merry race "God speed!"

How pleasant 'tis when brethren are agreed!

Hurrah! bad corpses turn into good dung,

To feed strange futures beautiful and young.

Hurrah! behold the progress of the waves

That mount to 'whelm the freedom which enslaves.

Progress be praised! for, though the inspired swine

Have won the hill-crest, there's, beyond, the brine!

  See, too, that other herd, which hurries the same way,

Bewitch'd, tails forward, faintly squeaking, "Stay!"

These, for the love of pence and places, slew

And to the common gutter cast

The corpse of Kingship, pleading, false, if they

Not did this, others would this do;

Mark, others those,

For planning this, their late-supplanted foes!

Now, when they thought to boast their better'd lot,

Their plagues wax hot.

See how they mildly court, 'mid bully and drab,

The stupid Cæsar they were sworn to stab!

o

The Northern Bog, too, now is on the slide.*

With a flung sod they late might bid it bide,

But not the whole world's force shall bid it back,

Because the Land it once crawls o'er

Is land no more;

And yet their arms hung marrowless and slack.

An Owl, when they would lift them, cried, "Tu-whoo!"

They fled, as Murder flees when none pursue;

The doom that faced their fleeing scared them not.

   —I only meant to jeer;

But wrath breaks down and blows away the crust

That caked mine eyes from scanning what is just,

And I see clear,

What better Bard hath seen

And sung 'mid pious hoots from all the unclean,

----

* This poem was written the year before the conclusion of Mr. Gladstone's Peace at Berlin.

That Heaven's smile

Sweetens to view the guerdon of the vile.

Not without frightful joy I watch the fate that's near;

For love of Land, which never cools,

Changes to love of vengeance, when the people change to

    fools.

  Now look no more! Enough of scorn!

Better relief from vainest tears is born.

Dear Land, that seem'd too sweetly wise,

Too sternly fair for aught that dies,

Past is thy proud and pleasant state,

That recent date

When, strong and single, in thy sovereign heart,

The thrones of thinking, hearing, sight,

The cunning hand, the knotted thew

Of lesser powers that heave and hew,

And each the smallest beneficial part,

And merest pore of breathing, beat,

Full and complete,

The great pulse of thy generous might,

Equal in inequality,

That soul of joy in low and high;

When not a churl but felt the Giant's heat,

Albeit he simply call'd it his,

Flush in his common labour with delight,

And not a village-Maiden's kiss

But was for this

More sweet,

And not a sorrow but did lightlier sigh,

And for its private self less greet,

The whilst that other so majestic self stood by!

Integrity so vast could well afford

To wear in working many a stain,

To pillory the cobbler vain

And license madness in a lord.

On that were all men well agreed;

And, if they did a thing,

Their strength was with them in their deed,

And from amongst them came the shout of a king !

   But, once let traitor coward meet,

Not Heaven itself can keep its feet.

Came knave who said to dastard, " Lo,

" The Deluge !" which but needed, " No !"

For all the Atlantic's threatening roar,

If men would bravely understand,

Is softly check'd for evermore

By a firm bar of sand.

But, dastard listening knave, who said,

" 'Twere juster were the Giant dead,

" That so yon bawlers may not miss

" To vote their own pot-belly'd bliss,"

All that is past !

We saw the slaying, and were not aghast.

But ne'er a sun, on village Groom and Bride,

Albeit they guess not how it is,

At Easter or at Whitsuntide,

But shines less gay for this!

XLVI.

THE CHILD'S PURCHASE.

A PROLOGUE.

As a young Child, whose Mother, for a jest,

To his own use a golden coin flings down,

Devises blythe how he may spend it best,

Or on a horse, a bride-cake, or a crown,

Till, wearied with his quest,

Nor liking altogether that nor this,

He gives it back for nothing but a kiss,

Endow'd so I

With golden speech, my choice of toys to buy,

And scanning power and pleasure and renown,

Till each in turn, with looking at, looks vain,

For her mouth's bliss,

To her who gave it give I it again.

 Ah, Lady elect,

Whom the Time's scorn has saved from its respect,

Would I had art

For uttering this which sings within my heart !

But, lo,

Thee to admire is all the art I know.

My Mother and God's ; Fountain of miracle !

Give me thereby some praise of thee to tell

In such a Song

As may my Guide severe and glad not wrong

Who never spake till thou'dst on him conferr'd

The right, convincing word !

Grant me the steady heat

Of thought wise, splendid, sweet,

Urged by the great, rejoicing wind that rings

With draft of unseen wings,

Making each phrase, for love and for delight,

Twinkle like Sirius on a frosty night!

Aid thou thine own dear fame, thou only Fair,

At whose petition meek

The Heavens themselves decree that, as it were,

They will be weak!

   Thou Speaker of all wisdom in a Word,

Thy Lord!

Speaker who thus could'st well afford

Thence to be silent;—ah, what silence that

Which had for prologue thy "Magnificat?"—

O, Silence full of wonders

More than by Moses in the Mount were heard,

More than were utter'd by the Seven Thunders;

Silence that crowns, unnoted, like the voiceless blue,

The loud world's varying view,

And in its holy heart the sense of all things ponders !

That acceptably I may speak of thee,

Ora pro me !

   Key-note and stop

Of the thunder-going chorus of sky-Powers ;

Essential drop

Distill'd from worlds of sweetest-savour'd flowers

To anoint with nuptial praise

The Head which for thy Beauty doff'd its rays,

And thee, in His exceeding glad descending, meant,

And Man's new days

Made of His deed the adorning accident !

Vast Nothingness of Self, fair female twin

Of Fulness, sucking all God's glory in !

(Ah, Mistress mine,

To nothing I have added only sin,

And yet would shine !)

Ora pro me !

Life's cradle and death's tomb !

To lie within whose womb,

There, with divine self-will infatuate,

Love-captive to the thing He did create,

Thy God did not abhor,

No more

Than Man, in Youth's high spousal-tide,

Abhors at last to touch

The strange lips of his long-procrastinating Bride ;

Nay, not the least imagined part as much !

Ora pro me !

My Lady, yea, the Lady of my Lord,

Who didst the first descry

The burning secret of virginity,

We know with what reward !

Prism whereby

Alone we see

Heav'n's light in its triplicity ;

Rainbow complex,

In bright distinction, of all beams of sex,

Shining for aye

In the simultaneous sky,

To One, thy Husband, Father, Son, and Brother,

Spouse blissful, Daughter, Sister, milk-sweet Mother ;

Ora pro me !

 Mildness, whom God obeys, obeying thyself

Him in thy joyful Saint, nigh lost to sight

In the great gulf

Of his own glory and thy neighbour light;

With whom thou wast as else with husband none

For perfect fruit of inmost amity ;

Who felt for thee

Such rapture of refusal that no kiss

Ever seal'd wedlock so conjoint with bliss ;

And whose good singular eternally

'Tis now, with nameless peace and vehemence,

To enjoy thy married smile,

That mystery of innocence ;

Ora pro me !

Sweet Girlhood without guile,

The extreme of God's creative energy ;

Sunshiny Peak of human personality ;

The world's sad aspirations' one Success ;

Bright Blush, that sav'st our shame from shamelessness ;

Chief Stone of stumbling ; Sign built in the way

To set the foolish everywhere a-bray ;

Hem of God's robe, which all who touch are heal'd ;

To which the outside Many honour yield

With a reward and grace

Unguess'd by the unwash'd boor that hails Him to His

    face,

Spurning the safe, ingratiant courtesy

Of suing Him by thee ;

Ora pro me !

Creature of God rather the sole than first;

Knot of the cord

Which binds together all and all unto their Lord;

Suppliant Omnipotence; best to the worst;

Our only Saviour from an abstract Christ

And Egypt's brick-kilns, where the lost crowd plods,

Blaspheming its false Gods;

Peace-beaming Star, by which shall come enticed,

Though nought thereof as yet they weet,

Unto thy Babe's small feet,

The Mighty, wand'ring disemparadised,

Like Lucifer, because to thee

They will not bend the knee;

Ora pro me !

Desire of Him whom all things else desire !

Bush aye with Him as He with thee on fire !

Neither in His great Deed nor on His throne—

O, folly of Love, the intense

Last culmination of Intelligence,—

Him seem'd it good that God should be alone!

Basking in unborn laughter of thy lips,

Ere the world was, with absolute delight

His Infinite reposed in thy Finite;

Well-match'd : He, universal being's Spring,

And thou, in whom are gather'd up the ends of everything!

Ora pro me!

   In season due, on His sweet-fearful bed,

Rock'd by an earthquake, curtain'd with eclipse,

Thou shar'd'st the spousal rapture of the sharp spear's head,

And thy bliss pale

Wrought for our boon what Eve's did for our bale;

Thereafter, holding a little thy soft breath,

Thou underwent'st the ceremony of death;

And, now, Queen-Wife,

Sitt'st at the right hand of the Lord of Life,

Who, of all bounty, craves for only fee

The glory of hearing it besought with smiles by thee !

Ora pro me !

   Mother, who lead'st me still by unknown ways,

Giving the gifts I know not how to ask,

Bless thou the work

Which, done, redeems my many wasted days,

Makes white the murk,

And crowns the few which thou wilt not dispraise,

When clear my Songs of Lady's graces rang,

And little guess'd I 'twas of thee I sang !

   Vainly, till now, my pray'rs would thee compel

To fire my verse with thy shy fame, too long

Shunning world-blazon of well-ponder'd song ;

But doubtful smiles, at last, 'mid thy denials lurk ;

From which I spell,

   " Humility and greatness grace the task

   " Which he who does it deems impossible !"